ACTIVE TREND TRADING
TRADE JOURNAL
& TRADING LOG

CLARIFY *Your* SYSTEM

SIMPLIFY *Your* PROCESS

MULTIPLY *Your* PROFITS

NAME

CONTACT

YEAR

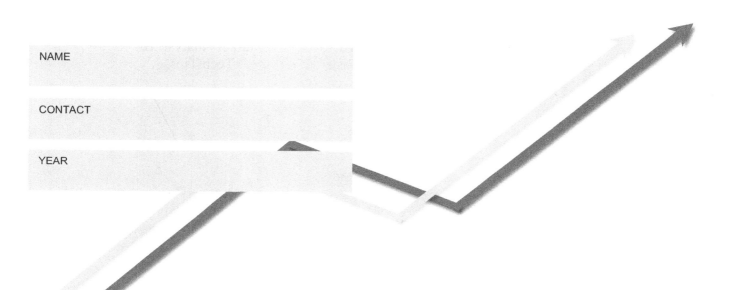

QUICK START

Thank you for choosing this Trade Journal from ActiveTrendTrading.com. We designed it specifically for the needs of our members as swing, trend, and options traders, with the goal of helping you achieve consistency and profitability. To begin, we recommend:

1   **Set Trading Rules**. Always trade with a set of objective rules that are written down. Write yours in the rules section. Refer to them often.

2   **Stick To A Routine.** Routines give you the best chance for good decision making. Write yours in the routine section. Schedule it in your calendar.

3   **Use Journal Pages to Plan Trades.** The Trade Checklist & Journal Pages are designed to walk you through the basics of most trade systems. Use them when preparing to trade, then follow up when the trade is complete.

4   **Track Progress in The Trade Log.** The Trade Log section is a quick reference to your trades and results.

Want to learn more about using this journal or get training on trading stocks and options? Visit ActiveTrendTrading.com/ and get free:

Video
Training

Curated
Watch Lists

Market Analysis &
Tech Tips

CONTENTS

LEGAL DISCLAIMER AND TERMS OF USE

HOW TO USE THIS TRADE JOURNAL

Thank you for choosing this Trade Journal from ActiveTrendTrading.com. We designed it specifically for the needs of our members as swing, trend, and options traders, with the goal of helping you achieve consistency and profitability.

Most traders struggle with that goal like someone lost in a fog. This journal helps provide clarity on all the information that isn't captured in your broker's trade confirmations or profit & loss reports: Your thoughts, emotions, and processes before and during a trade. As Mark Douglas suggests in the classic, *The Disciplined Trader*, if you know the market, but not yourself, you're going to struggle for consistent success. Journaling your perceptions during your trade decision process will allow you to track your own progress toward consistent action—and consistent action is what leads to consistent results.

In the spirit of our motto: "Clarify. Simplify. Multiply." this journal uses large, clear sections to keep information organized. It's simple to use to track your trading activity. And we hope that the extra diligence you give to your process will lead to multiplying your accounts.

There are three main sections to this book
1. Rules, Routines, & Goals
2. Trade Checklist & Journal Pages
3. Trade Log

In the first section, you'll see our rules as an example. You're free to use or adapt them for your style. Just be sure you write down your rules and refer to them often. We've also provided a sample routine.

Because we firmly believe in trading according to defined rules and a complete system, we've designed the trade checklist & journal pages to cover *The 5 Pillars of Any Successful System*: 1. What to Trade 2. When to Enter 3. When to Exit 4. Strategy, and 5. Expectation. They act like a pre-flight checklist for pilots, or a game plan for sports teams. You can learn more about the *5 Pillars* and the Active Trend Trading Rules at https://ActiveTrendTrading.com/five-pillars

The Trade Log is a short-hand, quick view of your trading results and progress.

TRADE CHECKLIST PAGES

DATE:
The date you are working through your decision process, or the date of the trade if you choose. Be consistent.

SYMBOL:
The stock, ETF, or other entity you're trading.

TRADE TYPE:
Long or short stock, or specific options or options spreads you are trading.

IS THIS TRADE COUNTER-TREND?
This check box is there for two reasons, as a rule-check (do your rules allow for counter-trend trades?), and for information to track your tendencies. It might be helpful to review charts after a trade is closed to see if you still agree with your choice.

TRIGGER:
What specific trigger in your rules is this trade based on?

SUPPORTING & OPPOSING EVIDENCE:
We often find that trade triggers occur in clusters. That is, price action signals, support/resistance, and oscillators will align for the best signals. This section is for the other evidence you see on the chart that either supports the trigger being valid or may be a hindrance to the trade.

HEADS UP:
Note any information, upcoming news, or chart data that you want to keep yourself aware of. Is earning next week? Is expiration coming? Is there resistance overhead?

ENTRY PLAN: This section lays out how you plan to enter the trade objectively.
- **ENTRY ORDER PRICE:** The initial price for your entry order. Change if the fill is different.
- **MAX STOP PRICE:** Your maximum stop price based on your rules. We have a maximum loss of 5% but usually use technical analysis for closer stops.
- **SIZE:** the number of shares or contracts you will trade based on the stop and your acceptable risk to your account. For help calculating this, we have a free tool you can find at https://ActiveTrendTrading.com/attsfreesignup
- **MAX $ LOSS:** This is here to help you prepare (mostly emotionally) for the chance that you might lose a certain dollar amount. If this amount makes you uncomfortable, consider lowering your trade size.

EXIT PLAN: This section lays out how you plan to exit the trade. It's best to have your plan ready before the trade is open to avoid impulsive reactions.
- TECHNICAL STOP: If you have a chart-based area to stop out instead of the max stop.
- EXIT TARGET/TRIGGER: Some people use technically determined price targets; others use mechanical exit triggers. List yours for this trade.
- TIME STOP: Will you exit if the trade goes nowhere? When?
- EST. RISK/REWARD: Based on your stop and targets, what's your risk/reward ratio? For example, are you risking $2 to earn $4? That's a 1:2 Risk/Reward.

ORDER/ALERTS PLACED? This is a process reminder. Circle whether you've placed alerts or orders and check the box.

RATE YOURSELF:

Self-accountability is challenging—but rewarding. It's one of those simple things that's hard to do. These small rating charts are there to keep you thinking about trading consistently and objectively, while giving you clues about your mindset while making decisions. If you answer low on question 1, journal your reasons for trading against your system. If you answer high on questions 2 or 3, journal about why those emotions are high.

NOTES/INSIGHTS/RESULTS:

Write any other notes or insights about the market, your trade, or your frame of mind. When the trade is closed, write down the results and whether you followed your exit plan. You don't have to write a lot, but try to be clear so you remember things.

"Don't dabble in stocks. Dig in and do some detective work."
WILLIAM O'NEIL

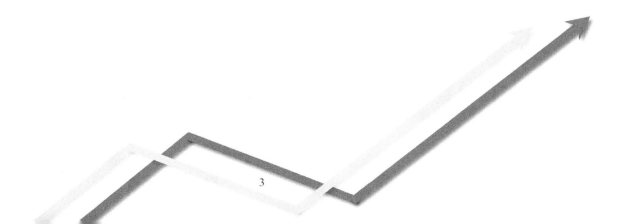

TRADE LOG PAGES:

The trade log pages are a shorthand record of your trading activity and will read similarly to your brokerage statements.

Symbol	Date Entry	Trade Type	Open Price	Close Price	#	Date Exit	Gain/Loss	Trigger or Note

- Symbol
- Date of entry
- Trade type (long/short stock or options info)
- Open price (we recommend entering negative numbers when buying to open (BTO), and positive numbers when selling to open (STO))
- Close price (positive numbers when selling to close (STC), negative when buying to close (BTC)),
- # of shares or contracts
- Date of exit
- Gain/Loss
- Trigger or note (or journal page).

If you would prefer to track this information on a spreadsheet, you can download a free at https://ActiveTrendTrading.com/attsfreesignup/ After tracking a large number of good trades, and by good trades we mean trades in which you followed your rules, you can develop a more accurate expectation for your trading system and personal performance.

"The four most expensive words in the English language are 'This time it's different.'"
SIR JOHN TEMPLETON

TRADING RULES

SAMPLE ACTIVE TREND TRADING RULES

These are the rules we've used to earn 31% or more, every year since 2012. Feel free to use them as is, or as a guide for your own rules. Try to keep them simple and clear.

What to Trade:

1. Leveraged ETF's, Stocks sorted from IBDs best lists of growth stocks
2. Stocks that pass IBD Stock Check Up with composite over 80 or EPS > 85
3. Stocks/Index ETFs Priced Over $10 with volume ≥ to 500K shares/day
4. Stocks/Index ETFs with Weekly Options (Desirable—not a must)
5. Stocks/Index ETFs from my personal and "Private Go-To" List
6. Stocks/Index ETFs with observable price patterns

When to Enter: At **Objectively** defined Action Points

1. Wait for TSI/Momentum Tick Up with crossover
2. Bounce or breakouts from moving averages; intraday (more aggressive) or closing
3. Trend line bounces or breaks
4. Support/Resistance bounces or breaks

Supplemental: With Convergence of Clues

Candlestick Patterns
Oscillator Divergences
Wait for the rebound or rejection of support/resistance – Don't Fade
Use consistent price trigger cushions (15-50 cents)

When to Exit: At **Objectively** defined Action Points

1. Stop Losses: 15-50 cents below swing low; OR Hard Stop Loss @ 4-7% loss from entry price based on stock or ETF
2. EMA Rule – a close below moving average that triggers the trade, OR a violation of the low of the candle that closes below the moving average.
3. Break of Trend Line: 15-50 cents
4. Profit Targets: 1/3 to 2/3 position at set technical targets. Adjust trailing stops.
5. Profit Stop after confirmed candlestick reversal signal
6. 2 Week Time Stop with no or little movement

Supplemental: With Convergence of Clues

What Strategy to Use: Long stocks and ETFs. Covered Calls, Directional Options, Spreads.

What to Expect: Cumulative Target: 40% ROI & 60% Winning Trades

MY TRADING RULES

What to Trade: What types of entities will you trade? Fundamental and technical characteristics, etc.

_____
_____
_____
_____
_____
_____

When to Enter: What are your entry rules or triggers?

_____
_____
_____
_____
_____
_____

When to Exit: What are your exit rules for stop losses and for profits?

_____
_____
_____
_____
_____
_____

What Strategy to Use: What strategies will you use? How will you determine when to use them?

_____
_____
_____
_____
_____

What to Expect: What are your expectations or broad goals for ROI or Win/Loss ratio?

_____
_____
_____
_____

MY TRADING RULES

"Once a rule is violated the slope has been greased!" DENNIS WILBORN

TRADING ROUTINES

Trading routines have one objective: Be Ready to Trade!

Just as professional athletes use routines for peak performance, a good routine can keep you trading efficiently and effectively.

An efficient routine answers 3 primary questions:

1. What are overall market conditions?
2. Are any of the stocks on your list near a trigger, or has one fired?
3. What must you do to be ready to trade potential triggers?

To be efficient, consider limiting the number of stocks on your watchlist and stop looking when you find a handful of potential opportunities.

Include routine actions:

	Time	What time you will prepare and what time you will trade?
	Review	After hours or pre-open review of market and watch list
	Setups	Check setups. Have any circumstances changed?
	Updates	Any upcoming news or announcements to keep in mind?
	Alerts/Orders	Check or place alerts and/or orders
	Journal & Log	Journal setups, trade details, and log closed trades
	Other	Any other personal routines or details

Our preference is to prepare after hours and use conditional orders to trade, removing impulse decisions and allowing us to live LIFE! Write out a trade routine that works for your lifestyle on the next page.

Put it in your schedule, try it out, and adjust as necessary.

MY TRADING ROUTINES

☑	Action/Time	Details

"To accomplish our goals, we must distill our dreams into daily actions." MICHAEL HYATT

TRADING GOALS

Trading goals encompass more than just returns. Almost more important are trading goals that aim at your own progress as a trader. Consider goals that target your consistency, education, and habits. After all, you're all you have control over.

Consider appropriate rewards if you meet the action goals you set.

To help you accomplish the goals you set, take on only a handful of things for the year, and chunk them down into smaller pieces for each quarter or month.

MY ANNUAL TRADING GOALS

☑	Goal	Target Date

"Plans fail for lack of counsel, but with many advisors they succeed." PROVERBS 15:22

SHORT-TERM TRADING GOALS

Q1:

☑	Goal	Target Date

Q2:

☑	Goal	Target Date

"Discipline is the bridge between goals and accomplishment." JIM ROHN

SHORT-TERM TRADING GOALS

Q3:

☑	Goal	Target Date

Q4:

☑	Goal	Target Date

"Fish see the bait, but not the hook; men see the profit, but not the peril". CHINESE PROVERB

"There is no Holy Grail of Trading— Only Rules and Tools."
DENNIS WILBORN

TRADE CHECKLIST & JOURNAL

Date:	Symbol:	Trade Type:

Is this a counter-trend trade? YES ☐ NO ☐ | Trigger:

+ Supporting Evidence +	**− Opposing Evidence −**

Heads Up:

Entry Plan		**Exit Plan**	
Entry Order Price:		Technical Stop:	
Max Stop Price:		Exit Target/Trigger:	
Size:		Time Stop:	
Max $ Loss		Est. Risk/Reward:	

Orders/Alerts Placed?   YES ☐   NO ☐   Notes/Insights/Results:

Rate Yourself - Does this trade:

1. Follow system rules?

    1   2   3   4   5

2. Result in fear/anxiety? (If high, why?)

    1   2   3   4   5

3. Spark "greed" or pride?

    1   2   3   4   5

TRADE CHECKLIST & JOURNAL

Date:	Symbol:	Trade Type:

Is this a counter-trend trade?   YES ☐   NO ☐

Trigger:

+ Supporting Evidence +	- Opposing Evidence -

Heads Up:

Entry Plan		Exit Plan	
Entry Order Price:		Technical Stop:	
Max Stop Price:		Exit Target/Trigger:	
Size:		Time Stop:	
Max $ Loss		Est. Risk/Reward:	

Orders/Alerts Placed?   YES ☐   NO ☐

Notes/Insights/Results:

Rate Yourself - Does this trade:

1. Follow system rules?

    1   2   3   4   5

2. Result in fear/anxiety? (If high, why?)

    1   2   3   4   5

3. Spark "greed" or pride?

    1   2   3   4   5

TRADE CHECKLIST & JOURNAL

Date:	Symbol:	Trade Type:

Is this a counter-trend trade? YES ☐ NO ☐ | Trigger:

+ Supporting Evidence +	- Opposing Evidence -

Heads Up:

Entry Plan		Exit Plan	
Entry Order Price:		Technical Stop:	
Max Stop Price:		Exit Target/Trigger:	
Size:		Time Stop:	
Max $ Loss		Est. Risk/Reward:	

Orders/Alerts Placed? YES ☐ NO ☐

Notes/Insights/Results:

Rate Yourself - Does this trade:

1. Follow system rules?

   1   2   3   4   5

2. Result in fear/anxiety? (If high, why?)

   1   2   3   4   5

3. Spark "greed" or pride?

   1   2   3   4   5

TRADE CHECKLIST & JOURNAL

Date:	Symbol:	Trade Type:

Is this a counter-trend trade?   YES ☐   NO ☐

Trigger:

+ Supporting Evidence +	- Opposing Evidence -

Heads Up:

Entry Plan		Exit Plan	
Entry Order Price:		Technical Stop:	
Max Stop Price:		Exit Target/Trigger:	
Size:		Time Stop:	
Max $ Loss		Est. Risk/Reward:	

Orders/Alerts Placed?   YES ☐   NO ☐

Rate Yourself - Does this trade:

1. Follow system rules?

   1   2   3   4   5

2. Result in fear/anxiety? (If high, why?)

   1   2   3   4   5

3. Spark "greed" or pride?

   1   2   3   4   5

Notes/Insights/Results:

TRADE CHECKLIST & JOURNAL

Date:	Symbol:	Trade Type:

Is this a counter-trend trade? YES ☐ NO ☐ | Trigger:

+ Supporting Evidence +	- Opposing Evidence -

Heads Up:

Entry Plan		Exit Plan	
Entry Order Price:		Technical Stop:	
Max Stop Price:		Exit Target/Trigger:	
Size:		Time Stop:	
Max $ Loss		Est. Risk/Reward:	

Orders/Alerts Placed?   YES ☐   NO ☐ | Notes/Insights/Results:

Rate Yourself - Does this trade:

1. Follow system rules?

   1   2   3   4   5

2. Result in fear/anxiety? (If high, why?)

   1   2   3   4   5

3. Spark "greed" or pride?

   1   2   3   4   5

TRADE CHECKLIST & JOURNAL

Date:	Symbol:	Trade Type:

Is this a counter-trend trade? YES ☐ NO ☐ | Trigger:

+ Supporting Evidence +	- Opposing Evidence -

Heads Up:

Entry Plan		Exit Plan	
Entry Order Price:		Technical Stop:	
Max Stop Price:		Exit Target/Trigger:	
Size:		Time Stop:	
Max $ Loss		Est. Risk/Reward:	

Orders/Alerts Placed? YES ☐ NO ☐ | Notes/Insights/Results:

Rate Yourself - Does this trade:

1. Follow system rules?

    1   2   3   4   5

2. Result in fear/anxiety? (If high, why?)

    1   2   3   4   5

3. Spark "greed" or pride?

    1   2   3   4   5

TRADE CHECKLIST & JOURNAL

Date:	Symbol:	Trade Type:

Is this a counter-trend trade? YES ☐ NO ☐   Trigger:

+ Supporting Evidence +	- Opposing Evidence -

Heads Up:

Entry Plan		Exit Plan	
Entry Order Price:		Technical Stop:	
Max Stop Price:		Exit Target/Trigger:	
Size:		Time Stop:	
Max $ Loss		Est. Risk/Reward:	

Orders/Alerts Placed?   YES ☐   NO ☐   Notes/Insights/Results:

Rate Yourself - Does this trade:

1. Follow system rules?

   1   2   3   4   5

2. Result in fear/anxiety? (If high, why?)

   1   2   3   4   5

3. Spark "greed" or pride?

   1   2   3   4   5

TRADE CHECKLIST & JOURNAL

Date:	Symbol:	Trade Type:

Is this a counter-trend trade?   YES ☐   NO ☐

Trigger:

+ Supporting Evidence +	- Opposing Evidence -

Heads Up:

Entry Plan		Exit Plan	
Entry Order Price:		Technical Stop:	
Max Stop Price:		Exit Target/Trigger:	
Size:		Time Stop:	
Max $ Loss		Est. Risk/Reward:	

Orders/Alerts Placed?   YES ☐   NO ☐

Notes/Insights/Results:

Rate Yourself - Does this trade:

1. Follow system rules?

   1   2   3   4   5

2. Result in fear/anxiety? (If high, why?)

   1   2   3   4   5

3. Spark "greed" or pride?

   1   2   3   4   5

TRADE CHECKLIST & JOURNAL

Date:	Symbol:	Trade Type:

Is this a counter-trend trade? YES ☐ NO ☐ | Trigger:

+ Supporting Evidence +	- Opposing Evidence -

Heads Up:

Entry Plan		Exit Plan	
Entry Order Price:		Technical Stop:	
Max Stop Price:		Exit Target/Trigger:	
Size:		Time Stop:	
Max $ Loss		Est. Risk/Reward:	

Orders/Alerts Placed?   YES ☐   NO ☐   Notes/Insights/Results:

Rate Yourself - Does this trade:

1. Follow system rules?

    1   2   3   4   5

2. Result in fear/anxiety? (If high, why?)

    1   2   3   4   5

3. Spark "greed" or pride?

    1   2   3   4   5

TRADE CHECKLIST & JOURNAL

Date:	Symbol:	Trade Type:

Is this a counter-trend trade? YES ☐ NO ☐ | Trigger: |

+ Supporting Evidence +	- Opposing Evidence -

Heads Up:

Entry Plan		Exit Plan	
Entry Order Price:		Technical Stop:	
Max Stop Price:		Exit Target/Trigger:	
Size:		Time Stop:	
Max $ Loss		Est. Risk/Reward:	

Orders/Alerts Placed? YES ☐ NO ☐   Notes/Insights/Results:

Rate Yourself - Does this trade:

1. Follow system rules?

   1   **2**   **3**   **4**   **5**

2. Result in fear/anxiety? (If high, why?)

   1   **2**   **3**   **4**   **5**

3. Spark "greed" or pride?

   1   **2**   **3**   **4**   **5**

"Markets are never wrong — opinions often are."
JESSE LIVERMORE

TRADE CHECKLIST & JOURNAL

Date:	Symbol:	Trade Type:

Is this a counter-trend trade?   YES ☐   NO ☐

Trigger:

+ Supporting Evidence +	- Opposing Evidence -

Heads Up:

Entry Plan		Exit Plan	
Entry Order Price:		Technical Stop:	
Max Stop Price:		Exit Target/Trigger:	
Size:		Time Stop:	
Max $ Loss		Est. Risk/Reward:	

Orders/Alerts Placed?   YES ☐   NO ☐

Notes/Insights/Results:

Rate Yourself - Does this trade:

1. Follow system rules?

    1   2   3   4   5

2. Result in fear/anxiety? (If high, why?)

    1   2   3   4   5

3. Spark "greed" or pride?

    1   2   3   4   5

TRADE CHECKLIST & JOURNAL

Date:	Symbol:	Trade Type:

Is this a counter-trend trade?   YES ☐   NO ☐

Trigger:

+ Supporting Evidence +	- Opposing Evidence -

Heads Up:

Entry Plan		Exit Plan	
Entry Order Price:		Technical Stop:	
Max Stop Price:		Exit Target/Trigger:	
Size:		Time Stop:	
Max $ Loss		Est. Risk/Reward:	

Orders/Alerts Placed?   YES ☐   NO ☐

Notes/Insights/Results:

Rate Yourself - Does this trade:

1. Follow system rules?

   1   2   3   4   5

2. Result in fear/anxiety? (If high, why?)

   1   2   3   4   5

3. Spark "greed" or pride?

   1   2   3   4   5

TRADE CHECKLIST & JOURNAL

Date:	Symbol:	Trade Type:

Is this a counter-trend trade?   YES ☐   NO ☐   Trigger:

+ Supporting Evidence +	- Opposing Evidence -

Heads Up:

Entry Plan		Exit Plan	
Entry Order Price:		Technical Stop:	
Max Stop Price:		Exit Target/Trigger:	
Size:		Time Stop:	
Max $ Loss		Est. Risk/Reward:	

Orders/Alerts Placed?   YES ☐   NO ☐   Notes/Insights/Results:

Rate Yourself - Does this trade:

1. Follow system rules?

   1   2   3   4   5

2. Result in fear/anxiety? (If high, why?)

   1   2   3   4   5

3. Spark "greed" or pride?

   1   2   3   4   5

TRADE CHECKLIST & JOURNAL

Date:	Symbol:	Trade Type:

Is this a counter-trend trade? YES ☐ NO ☐ | Trigger:

+ Supporting Evidence +	- Opposing Evidence -

Heads Up:

Entry Plan		Exit Plan	
Entry Order Price:		Technical Stop:	
Max Stop Price:		Exit Target/Trigger:	
Size:		Time Stop:	
Max $ Loss		Est. Risk/Reward:	

Orders/Alerts Placed?   YES ☐   NO ☐ | Notes/Insights/Results:

Rate Yourself - Does this trade:

1. Follow system rules?

    1   2   3   4   5

2. Result in fear/anxiety? (If high, why?)

    1   2   3   4   5

3. Spark "greed" or pride?

    1   2   3   4   5

TRADE CHECKLIST & JOURNAL

Date:	Symbol:	Trade Type:

Is this a counter-trend trade?   YES ☐   NO ☐   Trigger:

+ Supporting Evidence +	**- Opposing Evidence -**

Heads Up:

Entry Plan		**Exit Plan**	
Entry Order Price:		Technical Stop:	
Max Stop Price:		Exit Target/Trigger:	
Size:		Time Stop:	
Max $ Loss		Est. Risk/Reward:	

Orders/Alerts Placed?   YES ☐   NO ☐   Notes/Insights/Results:

Rate Yourself - Does this trade:

1. Follow system rules?

   1   2   3   4   5

2. Result in fear/anxiety? (If high, why?)

   1   2   3   4   5

3. Spark "greed" or pride?

   1   2   3   4   5

TRADE CHECKLIST & JOURNAL

Date:	Symbol:	Trade Type:

Is this a counter-trend trade?   YES ☐   NO ☐   Trigger:

+ Supporting Evidence +	- Opposing Evidence -

Heads Up:

Entry Plan		Exit Plan	
Entry Order Price:		Technical Stop:	
Max Stop Price:		Exit Target/Trigger:	
Size:		Time Stop:	
Max $ Loss		Est. Risk/Reward:	

Orders/Alerts Placed?   YES ☐   NO ☐   Notes/Insights/Results:

Rate Yourself - Does this trade:

1. Follow system rules?

   1   2   3   4   5

2. Result in fear/anxiety? (If high, why?)

   1   2   3   4   5

3. Spark "greed" or pride?

   1   2   3   4   5

TRADE CHECKLIST & JOURNAL

Date:	Symbol:	Trade Type:

Is this a counter-trend trade?   YES ☐   NO ☐ | Trigger:

+ Supporting Evidence +	- Opposing Evidence -

Heads Up:

Entry Plan		Exit Plan	
Entry Order Price:		Technical Stop:	
Max Stop Price:		Exit Target/Trigger:	
Size:		Time Stop:	
Max $ Loss		Est. Risk/Reward:	

Orders/Alerts Placed?   YES ☐   NO ☐   Notes/Insights/Results:

Rate Yourself - Does this trade:

1. Follow system rules?

   1   2   3   4   5

2. Result in fear/anxiety? (If high, why?)

   1   2   3   4   5

3. Spark "greed" or pride?

   1   2   3   4   5

TRADE CHECKLIST & JOURNAL

Date:	Symbol:	Trade Type:

Is this a counter-trend trade? YES ☐ NO ☐   Trigger:

+ Supporting Evidence +	- Opposing Evidence -

Heads Up:

Entry Plan		Exit Plan	
Entry Order Price:	.	Technical Stop:	
Max Stop Price:		Exit Target/Trigger:	
Size:		Time Stop:	
Max $ Loss		Est. Risk/Reward:	

Orders/Alerts Placed?   YES ☐   NO ☐   Notes/Insights/Results:

Rate Yourself - Does this trade:

1. Follow system rules?

   1   2   3   4   5

2. Result in fear/anxiety? (If high, why?)

   1   2   3   4   5

3. Spark "greed" or pride?

   1   2   3   4   5

TRADE CHECKLIST & JOURNAL

Date:	Symbol:	Trade Type:

Is this a counter-trend trade?   YES ☐   NO ☐ | Trigger:

+ Supporting Evidence +	**- Opposing Evidence -**

Heads Up:

Entry Plan		**Exit Plan**	
Entry Order Price:		Technical Stop:	
Max Stop Price:		Exit Target/Trigger:	
Size:		Time Stop:	
Max $ Loss		Est. Risk/Reward:	

Orders/Alerts Placed?   YES ☐   NO ☐

Notes/Insights/Results:

Rate Yourself - Does this trade:

1. Follow system rules?

   1   **2**   **3**   **4**   **5**

2. Result in fear/anxiety? (If high, why?)

   1   **2**   **3**   **4**   **5**

3. Spark "greed" or pride?

   1   **2**   **3**   **4**   **5**

TRADE CHECKLIST & JOURNAL

Date:	Symbol:	Trade Type:

Is this a counter-trend trade?   YES ☐   NO ☐ | Trigger: |

+ Supporting Evidence +	- Opposing Evidence -

Heads Up:

Entry Plan		Exit Plan	
Entry Order Price:		Technical Stop:	
Max Stop Price:		Exit Target/Trigger:	
Size:		Time Stop:	
Max $ Loss		Est. Risk/Reward:	

Orders/Alerts Placed?   YES ☐   NO ☐

Notes/Insights/Results:

Rate Yourself - Does this trade:

1. Follow system rules?

   1   2   3   4   5

2. Result in fear/anxiety? (If high, why?)

   1   2   3   4   5

3. Spark "greed" or pride?

   1   2   3   4   5

"Most trading errors come from a lack of patience and a compulsion to 'do something' even when nothing really needs to be done."
DENNIS WILBORN

TRADE CHECKLIST & JOURNAL

Date:	Symbol:	Trade Type:

Is this a counter-trend trade? YES ☐ NO ☐

Trigger:

+ Supporting Evidence +	- Opposing Evidence -

Heads Up:

Entry Plan		Exit Plan	
Entry Order Price:		Technical Stop:	
Max Stop Price:		Exit Target/Trigger:	
Size:		Time Stop:	
Max $ Loss		Est. Risk/Reward:	

Orders/Alerts Placed?   YES ☐   NO ☐

Notes/Insights/Results:

Rate Yourself - Does this trade:

1. Follow system rules?

   1   2   3   4   5

2. Result in fear/anxiety? (If high, why?)

   1   2   3   4   5

3. Spark "greed" or pride?

   1   2   3   4   5

TRADE CHECKLIST & JOURNAL

Date:	Symbol:	Trade Type:

Is this a counter-trend trade?   YES ☐   NO ☐ | Trigger:

+ Supporting Evidence +	- Opposing Evidence -

Heads Up:

Entry Plan		Exit Plan	
Entry Order Price:		Technical Stop:	
Max Stop Price:		Exit Target/Trigger:	
Size:		Time Stop:	
Max $ Loss		Est. Risk/Reward:	

Orders/Alerts Placed?   YES ☐   NO ☐

Notes/Insights/Results:

Rate Yourself - Does this trade:

1. Follow system rules?

   1   2   3   4   5

2. Result in fear/anxiety? (If high, why?)

   1   2   3   4   5

3. Spark "greed" or pride?

   1   2   3   4   5

TRADE CHECKLIST & JOURNAL

Date:	Symbol:	Trade Type:

Is this a counter-trend trade?   YES ☐   NO ☐   Trigger:

+ Supporting Evidence +	- Opposing Evidence -

Heads Up:

Entry Plan		Exit Plan	
Entry Order Price:		Technical Stop:	
Max Stop Price:		Exit Target/Trigger:	
Size:		Time Stop:	
Max $ Loss		Est. Risk/Reward:	

Orders/Alerts Placed?   YES ☐   NO ☐   Notes/Insights/Results:

Rate Yourself - Does this trade:

1. Follow system rules?

   1   2   3   4   5
   ●────────●────────●────────●────────●

2. Result in fear/anxiety? (If high, why?)

   1   2   3   4   5
   ●────────●────────●────────●────────●

3. Spark "greed" or pride?

   1   2   3   4   5
   ●────────●────────●────────●────────●

TRADE CHECKLIST & JOURNAL

Date:	Symbol:	Trade Type:

Is this a counter-trend trade?   YES ☐   NO ☐

Trigger:

+ Supporting Evidence +	- Opposing Evidence -

Heads Up:

Entry Plan		Exit Plan	
Entry Order Price:		Technical Stop:	
Max Stop Price:		Exit Target/Trigger:	
Size:		Time Stop:	
Max $ Loss		Est. Risk/Reward:	

Orders/Alerts Placed?   YES ☐   NO ☐

Rate Yourself - Does this trade:

1. Follow system rules?

   1   2   3   4   5

2. Result in fear/anxiety? (If high, why?)

   1   2   3   4   5

3. Spark "greed" or pride?

   1   2   3   4   5

Notes/Insights/Results:

TRADE CHECKLIST & JOURNAL

Date:

Symbol:

Trade Type:

Is this a counter-trend trade?   YES ☐   NO ☐

Trigger:

+ Supporting Evidence +	- Opposing Evidence -

Heads Up:

Entry Plan		Exit Plan	
Entry Order Price:		Technical Stop:	
Max Stop Price:		Exit Target/Trigger:	
Size:		Time Stop:	
Max $ Loss		Est. Risk/Reward:	

Orders/Alerts Placed?   YES ☐   NO ☐

Notes/Insights/Results:

Rate Yourself - Does this trade:

1. Follow system rules?

   1   2   3   4   5

2. Result in fear/anxiety? (If high, why?)

   1   2   3   4   5

3. Spark "greed" or pride?

   1   2   3   4   5

TRADE CHECKLIST & JOURNAL

Date:	Symbol:	Trade Type:

Is this a counter-trend trade? YES ☐ NO ☐ | Trigger:

+ Supporting Evidence +	- Opposing Evidence -

Heads Up:

Entry Plan		Exit Plan	
Entry Order Price:		Technical Stop:	
Max Stop Price:		Exit Target/Trigger:	
Size:		Time Stop:	
Max $ Loss		Est. Risk/Reward:	

Orders/Alerts Placed? YES ☐ NO ☐   Notes/Insights/Results:

Rate Yourself - Does this trade:

1. Follow system rules?

   1   2   3   4   5

2. Result in fear/anxiety? (If high, why?)

   1   2   3   4   5

3. Spark "greed" or pride?

   1   2   3   4   5

TRADE CHECKLIST & JOURNAL

Date:	Symbol:	Trade Type:

Is this a counter-trend trade?   YES ☐   NO ☐ | Trigger:

+ Supporting Evidence +	- Opposing Evidence -

Heads Up:

Entry Plan		Exit Plan	
Entry Order Price:		Technical Stop:	
Max Stop Price:		Exit Target/Trigger:	
Size:		Time Stop:	
Max $ Loss		Est. Risk/Reward:	

Orders/Alerts Placed?   YES ☐   NO ☐ | Notes/Insights/Results:

Rate Yourself - Does this trade:

1. Follow system rules?

   1   2   3   4   5

2. Result in fear/anxiety? (If high, why?)

   1   2   3   4   5

3. Spark "greed" or pride?

   1   2   3   4   5

TRADE CHECKLIST & JOURNAL

Date:	Symbol:	Trade Type:

Is this a counter-trend trade?   YES ☐   NO ☐ | Trigger:

+ Supporting Evidence +	- Opposing Evidence -

Heads Up:

Entry Plan		Exit Plan	
Entry Order Price:		Technical Stop:	
Max Stop Price:		Exit Target/Trigger:	
Size:		Time Stop:	
Max $ Loss		Est. Risk/Reward:	

Orders/Alerts Placed?   YES ☐   NO ☐ | Notes/Insights/Results:

Rate Yourself - Does this trade:

1. Follow system rules?
   1   2   3   4   5

2. Result in fear/anxiety? (If high, why?)
   1   2   3   4   5

3. Spark "greed" or pride?
   1   2   3   4   5

TRADE CHECKLIST & JOURNAL

Date:	Symbol:	Trade Type:

Is this a counter-trend trade? YES ☐ NO ☐ | Trigger:

+ Supporting Evidence +	- Opposing Evidence -

Heads Up:

Entry Plan		Exit Plan	
Entry Order Price:		Technical Stop:	
Max Stop Price:		Exit Target/Trigger:	
Size:		Time Stop:	
Max $ Loss		Est. Risk/Reward:	

Orders/Alerts Placed? YES ☐ NO ☐   Notes/Insights/Results:

Rate Yourself - Does this trade:

1. Follow system rules?

   1   2   3   4   5

2. Result in fear/anxiety? (If high, why?)

   1   2   3   4   5

3. Spark "greed" or pride?

   1   2   3   4   5

TRADE CHECKLIST & JOURNAL

Date:	Symbol:	Trade Type:

Is this a counter-trend trade? YES ☐ NO ☐

Trigger:

+ Supporting Evidence +	- Opposing Evidence -

Heads Up:

Entry Plan		Exit Plan	
Entry Order Price:		Technical Stop:	
Max Stop Price:		Exit Target/Trigger:	
Size:		Time Stop:	
Max $ Loss		Est. Risk/Reward:	

Orders/Alerts Placed? YES ☐ NO ☐

Notes/Insights/Results:

Rate Yourself - Does this trade:

1. Follow system rules?

   1   2   3   4   5

2. Result in fear/anxiety? (If high, why?)

   1   2   3   4   5

3. Spark "greed" or pride?

   1   2   3   4   5

"If you don't know precisely what signal is yours and how you will size and manage your position—STOP TRADING!"
PETER BRANDT

TRADE CHECKLIST & JOURNAL

Date:	Symbol:	Trade Type:

Is this a counter-trend trade?   YES ☐   NO ☐ | Trigger:

+ Supporting Evidence +	- Opposing Evidence -

Heads Up:

Entry Plan		Exit Plan	
Entry Order Price:		Technical Stop:	
Max Stop Price:		Exit Target/Trigger:	
Size:		Time Stop:	
Max $ Loss		Est. Risk/Reward:	

Orders/Alerts Placed?   YES ☐   NO ☐ | Notes/Insights/Results:

Rate Yourself - Does this trade:

1. Follow system rules?

   1   2   3   4   5

2. Result in fear/anxiety? (If high, why?)

   1   2   3   4   5

3. Spark "greed" or pride?

   1   2   3   4   5

TRADE CHECKLIST & JOURNAL

Date:	Symbol:	Trade Type:

Is this a counter-trend trade?   YES ☐   NO ☐   Trigger:

+ Supporting Evidence +	- Opposing Evidence -

Heads Up:

Entry Plan		Exit Plan	
Entry Order Price:		Technical Stop:	
Max Stop Price:		Exit Target/Trigger:	
Size:		Time Stop:	
Max $ Loss		Est. Risk/Reward:	

Orders/Alerts Placed?   YES ☐   NO ☐   Notes/Insights/Results:

Rate Yourself - Does this trade:

1. Follow system rules?

   1   2   3   4   5

2. Result in fear/anxiety? (If high, why?)

   1   2   3   4   5

3. Spark "greed" or pride?

   1   2   3   4   5

TRADE CHECKLIST & JOURNAL

Date:	Symbol:	Trade Type:

Is this a counter-trend trade?   YES ☐   NO ☐   Trigger:

+ Supporting Evidence +	**– Opposing Evidence –**

Heads Up:

Entry Plan		**Exit Plan**	
Entry Order Price:		Technical Stop:	
Max Stop Price:		Exit Target/Trigger:	
Size:		Time Stop:	
Max $ Loss		Est. Risk/Reward:	

Orders/Alerts Placed?   YES ☐   NO ☐

Notes/Insights/Results:

Rate Yourself - Does this trade:

1. Follow system rules?

   1   2   3   4   5

2. Result in fear/anxiety? (If high, why?)

   1   2   3   4   5

3. Spark "greed" or pride?

   1   2   3   4   5

TRADE CHECKLIST & JOURNAL

Date:	Symbol:	Trade Type:

Is this a counter-trend trade?   YES ☐   NO ☐   Trigger:

+ Supporting Evidence +	- Opposing Evidence -

Heads Up:

Entry Plan		Exit Plan	
Entry Order Price:		Technical Stop:	
Max Stop Price:		Exit Target/Trigger:	
Size:		Time Stop:	
Max $ Loss		Est. Risk/Reward:	

Orders/Alerts Placed?   YES ☐   NO ☐   Notes/Insights/Results:

Rate Yourself - Does this trade:

1. Follow system rules?

    1   **2**   **3**   **4**   **5**

2. Result in fear/anxiety? (If high, why?)

    1   **2**   **3**   **4**   **5**

3. Spark "greed" or pride?

    1   **2**   **3**   **4**   **5**

TRADE CHECKLIST & JOURNAL

Date:	Symbol:	Trade Type:

Is this a counter-trend trade?   YES ☐   NO ☐ | Trigger:

+ Supporting Evidence +	- Opposing Evidence -

Heads Up:

Entry Plan		Exit Plan	
Entry Order Price:		Technical Stop:	
Max Stop Price:		Exit Target/Trigger:	
Size:		Time Stop:	
Max $ Loss		Est. Risk/Reward:	

Orders/Alerts Placed?   YES ☐   NO ☐

Notes/Insights/Results:

Rate Yourself - Does this trade:

1. Follow system rules?

   1   2   3   4   5

2. Result in fear/anxiety? (If high, why?)

   1   2   3   4   5

3. Spark "greed" or pride?

   1   2   3   4   5

TRADE CHECKLIST & JOURNAL

Date:	Symbol:	Trade Type:

Is this a counter-trend trade? YES ☐ NO ☐ | Trigger:

+ Supporting Evidence +	- Opposing Evidence -

Heads Up:

Entry Plan		Exit Plan	
Entry Order Price:		Technical Stop:	
Max Stop Price:		Exit Target/Trigger:	
Size:		Time Stop:	
Max $ Loss		Est. Risk/Reward:	

Orders/Alerts Placed?   YES ☐   NO ☐ | Notes/Insights/Results:

Rate Yourself - Does this trade:

1. Follow system rules?

    1   2   3   4   5

2. Result in fear/anxiety? (If high, why?)

    1   2   3   4   5

3. Spark "greed" or pride?

    1   2   3   4   5

TRADE CHECKLIST & JOURNAL

Date:	Symbol:	Trade Type:

Is this a counter-trend trade?   YES ☐   NO ☐ | Trigger: |

+ Supporting Evidence +	- Opposing Evidence -

Heads Up:

Entry Plan		Exit Plan	
Entry Order Price:		Technical Stop:	
Max Stop Price:		Exit Target/Trigger:	
Size:		Time Stop:	
Max $ Loss		Est. Risk/Reward:	

Orders/Alerts Placed?   YES ☐   NO ☐

Notes/Insights/Results:

Rate Yourself - Does this trade:

1. Follow system rules?

   1   2   3   4   5

2. Result in fear/anxiety? (If high, why?)

   1   2   3   4   5

3. Spark "greed" or pride?

   1   2   3   4   5

TRADE CHECKLIST & JOURNAL

Date:	Symbol:	Trade Type:

Is this a counter-trend trade? YES ☐ NO ☐ | Trigger:

+ Supporting Evidence +	- Opposing Evidence -

Heads Up:

Entry Plan		Exit Plan	
Entry Order Price:		Technical Stop:	
Max Stop Price:		Exit Target/Trigger:	
Size:		Time Stop:	
Max $ Loss		Est. Risk/Reward:	

Orders/Alerts Placed? YES ☐ NO ☐ | Notes/Insights/Results:

Rate Yourself - Does this trade:

1. Follow system rules?

   1   2   3   4   5

2. Result in fear/anxiety? (If high, why?)

   1   2   3   4   5

3. Spark "greed" or pride?

   1   2   3   4   5

TRADE CHECKLIST & JOURNAL

Date:	Symbol:	Trade Type:

Is this a counter-trend trade?   YES ☐   NO ☐ | Trigger: |

+ Supporting Evidence +	**- Opposing Evidence -**

Heads Up:

Entry Plan		**Exit Plan**	
Entry Order Price:		Technical Stop:	
Max Stop Price:		Exit Target/Trigger:	
Size:		Time Stop:	
Max $ Loss		Est. Risk/Reward:	

Orders/Alerts Placed?   YES ☐   NO ☐

Rate Yourself - Does this trade:

1. Follow system rules?
   1   2   3   4   5

2. Result in fear/anxiety? (If high, why?)
   1   2   3   4   5

3. Spark "greed" or pride?
   1   2   3   4   5

Notes/Insights/Results:

TRADE CHECKLIST & JOURNAL

Date:	Symbol:	Trade Type:

Is this a counter-trend trade?   YES ☐   NO ☐ | Trigger: |

+ Supporting Evidence +	- Opposing Evidence -

Heads Up:

Entry Plan		Exit Plan	
Entry Order Price:		Technical Stop:	
Max Stop Price:		Exit Target/Trigger:	
Size:		Time Stop:	
Max $ Loss		Est. Risk/Reward:	

Orders/Alerts Placed?   YES ☐   NO ☐

Notes/Insights/Results:

Rate Yourself - Does this trade:

1. Follow system rules?

    1   2   3   4   5

2. Result in fear/anxiety? (If high, why?)

    1   2   3   4   5

3. Spark "greed" or pride?

    1   2   3   4   5

"You should have a clear target where to sell if the market moves against you.
And you must obey your rules!"
JESSE LIVERMORE

TRADE CHECKLIST & JOURNAL

Date:	Symbol:	Trade Type:

Is this a counter-trend trade? YES ☐ NO ☐   Trigger:

+ Supporting Evidence +	- Opposing Evidence -

Heads Up:

Entry Plan		Exit Plan	
Entry Order Price:		Technical Stop:	
Max Stop Price:		Exit Target/Trigger:	
Size:		Time Stop:	
Max $ Loss		Est. Risk/Reward:	

Orders/Alerts Placed?   YES ☐   NO ☐   Notes/Insights/Results:

Rate Yourself - Does this trade:

1. Follow system rules?

   1   2   3   4   5

2. Result in fear/anxiety? (If high, why?)

   1   2   3   4   5

3. Spark "greed" or pride?

   1   2   3   4   5

TRADE CHECKLIST & JOURNAL

Date:	Symbol:	Trade Type:

Is this a counter-trend trade?   YES ☐   NO ☐ | Trigger:

+ Supporting Evidence +	- Opposing Evidence -

Heads Up:

Entry Plan		Exit Plan	
Entry Order Price:		Technical Stop:	
Max Stop Price:		Exit Target/Trigger:	
Size:		Time Stop:	
Max $ Loss		Est. Risk/Reward:	

Orders/Alerts Placed?   YES ☐   NO ☐ | Notes/Insights/Results:

Rate Yourself - Does this trade:

1. Follow system rules?

   1   2   3   4   5

2. Result in fear/anxiety? (If high, why?)

   1   2   3   4   5

3. Spark "greed" or pride?

   1   2   3   4   5

TRADE CHECKLIST & JOURNAL

Date:	Symbol:	Trade Type:

Is this a counter-trend trade?   YES ☐   NO ☐   Trigger:

+ Supporting Evidence +	- Opposing Evidence -

Heads Up:

Entry Plan		Exit Plan	
Entry Order Price:		Technical Stop:	
Max Stop Price:		Exit Target/Trigger:	
Size:		Time Stop:	
Max $ Loss		Est. Risk/Reward:	

Orders/Alerts Placed?   YES ☐   NO ☐   Notes/Insights/Results:

Rate Yourself - Does this trade:

1. Follow system rules?

   1   2   3   4   5

2. Result in fear/anxiety? (If high, why?)

   1   2   3   4   5

3. Spark "greed" or pride?

   1   2   3   4   5

TRADE CHECKLIST & JOURNAL

Date:	Symbol:	Trade Type:

Is this a counter-trend trade? YES ☐ NO ☐

Trigger:

+ Supporting Evidence +	- Opposing Evidence -

Heads Up:

Entry Plan		Exit Plan	
Entry Order Price:		Technical Stop:	
Max Stop Price:		Exit Target/Trigger:	
Size:		Time Stop:	
Max $ Loss		Est. Risk/Reward:	

Orders/Alerts Placed?   YES ☐   NO ☐

Notes/Insights/Results:

Rate Yourself - Does this trade:

1. Follow system rules?

   1   2   3   4   5

2. Result in fear/anxiety? (If high, why?)

   1   2   3   4   5

3. Spark "greed" or pride?

   1   2   3   4   5

TRADE CHECKLIST & JOURNAL

Date:	Symbol:	Trade Type:

Is this a counter-trend trade?   YES ☐   NO ☐ | Trigger: |

+ Supporting Evidence +	- Opposing Evidence -

Heads Up:

Entry Plan		Exit Plan	
Entry Order Price:		Technical Stop:	
Max Stop Price:		Exit Target/Trigger:	
Size:		Time Stop:	
Max $ Loss		Est. Risk/Reward:	

Orders/Alerts Placed?   YES ☐   NO ☐   Notes/Insights/Results:

Rate Yourself - Does this trade:

1. Follow system rules?

   1   2   3   4   5

2. Result in fear/anxiety? (If high, why?)

   1   2   3   4   5

3. Spark "greed" or pride?

   1   2   3   4   5

TRADE CHECKLIST & JOURNAL

Date:	Symbol:	Trade Type:

Is this a counter-trend trade? YES ☐ NO ☐   Trigger:

+ Supporting Evidence +	- Opposing Evidence -

Heads Up:

Entry Plan		Exit Plan	
Entry Order Price:		Technical Stop:	
Max Stop Price:		Exit Target/Trigger:	
Size:		Time Stop:	
Max $ Loss		Est. Risk/Reward:	

Orders/Alerts Placed?   YES ☐   NO ☐   Notes/Insights/Results:

Rate Yourself - Does this trade:

1. Follow system rules?

   1   2   3   4   5

2. Result in fear/anxiety? (If high, why?)

   1   2   3   4   5

3. Spark "greed" or pride?

   1   2   3   4   5

TRADE CHECKLIST & JOURNAL

Date:	Symbol:	Trade Type:

Is this a counter-trend trade?   YES ☐   NO ☐

Trigger:

+ Supporting Evidence +	- Opposing Evidence -

Heads Up:

Entry Plan		Exit Plan	
Entry Order Price:		Technical Stop:	
Max Stop Price:		Exit Target/Trigger:	
Size:		Time Stop:	
Max $ Loss		Est. Risk/Reward:	

Orders/Alerts Placed?   YES ☐   NO ☐

Notes/Insights/Results:

Rate Yourself - Does this trade:

1. Follow system rules?

   1   2   3   4   5

2. Result in fear/anxiety? (If high, why?)

   1   2   3   4   5

3. Spark "greed" or pride?

   1   2   3   4   5

TRADE CHECKLIST & JOURNAL

Date:	Symbol:	Trade Type:

Is this a counter-trend trade?   YES ☐   NO ☐   Trigger:

+ Supporting Evidence +	- Opposing Evidence -

Heads Up:

Entry Plan		Exit Plan	
Entry Order Price:		Technical Stop:	
Max Stop Price:		Exit Target/Trigger:	
Size:		Time Stop:	
Max $ Loss		Est. Risk/Reward:	

Orders/Alerts Placed?   YES ☐   NO ☐   Notes/Insights/Results:

Rate Yourself - Does this trade:

1. Follow system rules?

   1   2   3   4   5

2. Result in fear/anxiety? (If high, why?)

   1   2   3   4   5

3. Spark "greed" or pride?

   1   2   3   4   5

TRADE CHECKLIST & JOURNAL

Date:	Symbol:	Trade Type:

Is this a counter-trend trade?   YES ☐   NO ☐ | Trigger:

+ Supporting Evidence +	- Opposing Evidence -

Heads Up:

Entry Plan		Exit Plan	
Entry Order Price:		Technical Stop:	
Max Stop Price:		Exit Target/Trigger:	
Size:		Time Stop:	
Max $ Loss		Est. Risk/Reward:	

Orders/Alerts Placed?   YES ☐   NO ☐

Notes/Insights/Results:

Rate Yourself - Does this trade:

1. Follow system rules?

   1   2   3   4   5

2. Result in fear/anxiety? (If high, why?)

   1   2   3   4   5

3. Spark "greed" or pride?

   1   2   3   4   5

TRADE CHECKLIST & JOURNAL

Date:	Symbol:	Trade Type:

Is this a counter-trend trade?   YES ☐   NO ☐

Trigger:

+ Supporting Evidence +	- Opposing Evidence -

Heads Up:

Entry Plan		Exit Plan	
Entry Order Price:		Technical Stop:	
Max Stop Price:		Exit Target/Trigger:	
Size:		Time Stop:	
Max $ Loss		Est. Risk/Reward:	

Orders/Alerts Placed?   YES ☐   NO ☐

Notes/Insights/Results:

Rate Yourself - Does this trade:

1. Follow system rules?

   1   2   3   4   5

2. Result in fear/anxiety? (If high, why?)

   1   2   3   4   5

3. Spark "greed" or pride?

   1   2   3   4   5

"Learn to focus on the process—the profits will follow!"
DENNIS WILBORN

TRADE CHECKLIST & JOURNAL

Date:	Symbol:	Trade Type:

Is this a counter-trend trade? YES ☐ NO ☐

Trigger:

+ Supporting Evidence +	**- Opposing Evidence -**

Heads Up:

Entry Plan		**Exit Plan**	
Entry Order Price:		Technical Stop:	
Max Stop Price:		Exit Target/Trigger:	
Size:		Time Stop:	
Max $ Loss		Est. Risk/Reward:	

Orders/Alerts Placed? YES ☐ NO ☐

Notes/Insights/Results:

Rate Yourself - Does this trade:

1. Follow system rules?

   1   2   3   4   5

2. Result in fear/anxiety? (If high, why?)

   1   2   3   4   5

3. Spark "greed" or pride?

   1   2   3   4   5

TRADE CHECKLIST & JOURNAL

Date:	Symbol:	Trade Type:

Is this a counter-trend trade? YES ☐ NO ☐ Trigger:

+ Supporting Evidence +	- Opposing Evidence -

Heads Up:

Entry Plan		Exit Plan	
Entry Order Price:		Technical Stop:	
Max Stop Price:		Exit Target/Trigger:	
Size:		Time Stop:	
Max $ Loss		Est. Risk/Reward:	

Orders/Alerts Placed?   YES ☐   NO ☐   Notes/Insights/Results:

Rate Yourself - Does this trade:

1. Follow system rules?

    1   2   3   4   5

2. Result in fear/anxiety? (If high, why?)

    1   2   3   4   5

3. Spark "greed" or pride?

    1   2   3   4   5

TRADE CHECKLIST & JOURNAL

Date:	Symbol:	Trade Type:

Is this a counter-trend trade?   YES ☐   NO ☐ | Trigger:

+ Supporting Evidence +	- Opposing Evidence -

Heads Up:

Entry Plan		Exit Plan	
Entry Order Price:		Technical Stop:	
Max Stop Price:		Exit Target/Trigger:	
Size:		Time Stop:	
Max $ Loss		Est. Risk/Reward:	

Orders/Alerts Placed?   YES ☐   NO ☐

Notes/Insights/Results:

Rate Yourself - Does this trade:

1. Follow system rules?

   1   2   3   4   5

2. Result in fear/anxiety? (If high, why?)

   1   2   3   4   5

3. Spark "greed" or pride?

   1   2   3   4   5

TRADE CHECKLIST & JOURNAL

Date:	Symbol:	Trade Type:

Is this a counter-trend trade?   YES ☐   NO ☐ | Trigger:

+ Supporting Evidence +	- Opposing Evidence -

Heads Up:

Entry Plan		Exit Plan	
Entry Order Price:		Technical Stop:	
Max Stop Price:		Exit Target/Trigger:	
Size:		Time Stop:	
Max $ Loss		Est. Risk/Reward:	

Orders/Alerts Placed?   YES ☐   NO ☐ | Notes/Insights/Results:

Rate Yourself - Does this trade:

1. Follow system rules?

   1   2   3   4   5

2. Result in fear/anxiety? (If high, why?)

   1   2   3   4   5

3. Spark "greed" or pride?

   1   2   3   4   5

TRADE CHECKLIST & JOURNAL

Date:	Symbol:	Trade Type:

Is this a counter-trend trade?   YES ☐   NO ☐   Trigger:

+ Supporting Evidence +	- Opposing Evidence -

Heads Up:

Entry Plan		Exit Plan	
Entry Order Price:		Technical Stop:	
Max Stop Price:		Exit Target/Trigger:	
Size:		Time Stop:	
Max $ Loss		Est. Risk/Reward:	

Orders/Alerts Placed?   YES ☐   NO ☐   Notes/Insights/Results:

Rate Yourself - Does this trade:

1. Follow system rules?

   1   2   3   4   5

2. Result in fear/anxiety? (If high, why?)

   1   2   3   4   5

3. Spark "greed" or pride?

   1   2   3   4   5

TRADE CHECKLIST & JOURNAL

Date:	Symbol:	Trade Type:

Is this a counter-trend trade?   YES ☐   NO ☐ | Trigger:

+ Supporting Evidence +	- Opposing Evidence -

Heads Up:

Entry Plan		Exit Plan	
Entry Order Price:		Technical Stop:	
Max Stop Price:		Exit Target/Trigger:	
Size:		Time Stop:	
Max $ Loss		Est. Risk/Reward:	

Orders/Alerts Placed?   YES ☐   NO ☐   Notes/Insights/Results:

Rate Yourself - Does this trade:

1. Follow system rules?

   1   2   3   4   5

2. Result in fear/anxiety? (If high, why?)

   1   2   3   4   5

3. Spark "greed" or pride?

   1   2   3   4   5

TRADE CHECKLIST & JOURNAL

Date:	Symbol:	Trade Type:

Is this a counter-trend trade? YES ☐ NO ☐ | Trigger:

+ Supporting Evidence +	- Opposing Evidence -

Heads Up:

Entry Plan		Exit Plan	
Entry Order Price:		Technical Stop:	
Max Stop Price:		Exit Target/Trigger:	
Size:		Time Stop:	
Max $ Loss		Est. Risk/Reward:	

Orders/Alerts Placed?   YES ☐   NO ☐

Notes/Insights/Results:

Rate Yourself - Does this trade:

1. Follow system rules?

   1   2   3   4   5

2. Result in fear/anxiety? (If high, why?)

   1   2   3   4   5

3. Spark "greed" or pride?

   1   2   3   4   5

TRADE CHECKLIST & JOURNAL

Date:	Symbol:	Trade Type:

Is this a counter-trend trade?   YES ☐   NO ☐   Trigger:

+ Supporting Evidence +	- Opposing Evidence -

Heads Up:

Entry Plan		Exit Plan	
Entry Order Price:		Technical Stop:	
Max Stop Price:		Exit Target/Trigger:	
Size:		Time Stop:	
Max $ Loss		Est. Risk/Reward:	

Orders/Alerts Placed?   YES ☐   NO ☐   Notes/Insights/Results:

Rate Yourself - Does this trade:

1. Follow system rules?

   1   2   3   4   5

2. Result in fear/anxiety? (If high, why?)

   1   2   3   4   5

3. Spark "greed" or pride?

   1   2   3   4   5

TRADE CHECKLIST & JOURNAL

Date:	Symbol:	Trade Type:

Is this a counter-trend trade?   YES ☐   NO ☐

Trigger:

+ Supporting Evidence +	- Opposing Evidence -

Heads Up:

Entry Plan		Exit Plan	
Entry Order Price:		Technical Stop:	
Max Stop Price:		Exit Target/Trigger:	
Size:		Time Stop:	
Max $ Loss		Est. Risk/Reward:	

Orders/Alerts Placed?   YES ☐   NO ☐

Notes/Insights/Results:

Rate Yourself - Does this trade:

1. Follow system rules?

   1   2   3   4   5

2. Result in fear/anxiety? (If high, why?)

   1   2   3   4   5

3. Spark "greed" or pride?

   1   2   3   4   5

TRADE CHECKLIST & JOURNAL

Date:	Symbol:	Trade Type:

Is this a counter-trend trade?   YES ☐   NO ☐ | Trigger:

+ Supporting Evidence +	- Opposing Evidence -

Heads Up:

Entry Plan		Exit Plan	
Entry Order Price:		Technical Stop:	
Max Stop Price:		Exit Target/Trigger:	
Size:		Time Stop:	
Max $ Loss		Est. Risk/Reward:	

Orders/Alerts Placed?   YES ☐   NO ☐   Notes/Insights/Results:

Rate Yourself - Does this trade:

1. Follow system rules?

    1   2   3   4   5

2. Result in fear/anxiety? (If high, why?)

    1   2   3   4   5

3. Spark "greed" or pride?

    1   2   3   4   5

"The whole secret to winning big in the stock market is not to be right all the time, but to lose the least amount possible when you're wrong."
WILLIAM O'NEIL

TRADE CHECKLIST & JOURNAL

Date:	Symbol:	Trade Type:

Is this a counter-trend trade?   YES ☐   NO ☐ | Trigger:

+ Supporting Evidence +	- Opposing Evidence -

Heads Up:

Entry Plan		Exit Plan	
Entry Order Price:		Technical Stop:	
Max Stop Price:		Exit Target/Trigger:	
Size:		Time Stop:	
Max $ Loss		Est. Risk/Reward:	

Orders/Alerts Placed?   YES ☐   NO ☐   Notes/Insights/Results:

Rate Yourself - Does this trade:

1. Follow system rules?

   1   2   3   4   5

2. Result in fear/anxiety? (If high, why?)

   1   2   3   4   5

3. Spark "greed" or pride?

   1   2   3   4   5

TRADE CHECKLIST & JOURNAL

Date:	Symbol:	Trade Type:

Is this a counter-trend trade?   YES ☐   NO ☐ | Trigger:

+ Supporting Evidence +	- Opposing Evidence -

Heads Up:

Entry Plan		Exit Plan	
Entry Order Price:		Technical Stop:	
Max Stop Price:		Exit Target/Trigger:	
Size:		Time Stop:	
Max $ Loss		Est. Risk/Reward:	

Orders/Alerts Placed?   YES ☐   NO ☐

Notes/Insights/Results:

Rate Yourself - Does this trade:

1. Follow system rules?

   1   2   3   4   5

2. Result in fear/anxiety? (If high, why?)

   1   2   3   4   5

3. Spark "greed" or pride?

   1   2   3   4   5

TRADE CHECKLIST & JOURNAL

Date:	Symbol:	Trade Type:

Is this a counter-trend trade?   YES ☐   NO ☐ | Trigger:

+ Supporting Evidence +	- Opposing Evidence -

Heads Up:

Entry Plan		Exit Plan	
Entry Order Price:		Technical Stop:	
Max Stop Price:		Exit Target/Trigger:	
Size:		Time Stop:	
Max $ Loss		Est. Risk/Reward:	

Orders/Alerts Placed?   YES ☐   NO ☐

Notes/Insights/Results:

Rate Yourself - Does this trade:

1. Follow system rules?
   1   2   3   4   5

2. Result in fear/anxiety? (If high, why?)
   1   2   3   4   5

3. Spark "greed" or pride?
   1   2   3   4   5

TRADE CHECKLIST & JOURNAL

Date:	Symbol:	Trade Type:

Is this a counter-trend trade?   YES ☐   NO ☐ | Trigger: |

+ Supporting Evidence +	- Opposing Evidence -

Heads Up:

Entry Plan		Exit Plan	
Entry Order Price:		Technical Stop:	
Max Stop Price:		Exit Target/Trigger:	
Size:		Time Stop:	
Max $ Loss		Est. Risk/Reward:	

Orders/Alerts Placed?   YES ☐   NO ☐   Notes/Insights/Results:

Rate Yourself - Does this trade:

1. Follow system rules?

   1   2   3   4   5

2. Result in fear/anxiety? (If high, why?)

   1   2   3   4   5

3. Spark "greed" or pride?

   1   2   3   4   5

TRADE CHECKLIST & JOURNAL

Date:	Symbol:	Trade Type:

Is this a counter-trend trade? YES ☐ NO ☐   Trigger:

+ Supporting Evidence +	**- Opposing Evidence -**

Heads Up:

Entry Plan		**Exit Plan**	
Entry Order Price:		Technical Stop:	
Max Stop Price:		Exit Target/Trigger:	
Size:		Time Stop:	
Max $ Loss		Est. Risk/Reward:	

Orders/Alerts Placed?   YES ☐   NO ☐   Notes/Insights/Results:

Rate Yourself - Does this trade:

1. Follow system rules?

   1   2   3   4   5

2. Result in fear/anxiety? (If high, why?)

   1   2   3   4   5

3. Spark "greed" or pride?

   1   2   3   4   5

TRADE CHECKLIST & JOURNAL

Date:	Symbol:	Trade Type:

Is this a counter-trend trade?   YES ☐   NO ☐   Trigger:

+ Supporting Evidence +	- Opposing Evidence -

Heads Up:

Entry Plan		Exit Plan	
Entry Order Price:		Technical Stop:	
Max Stop Price:		Exit Target/Trigger:	
Size:		Time Stop:	
Max $ Loss		Est. Risk/Reward:	

Orders/Alerts Placed?   YES ☐   NO ☐

Notes/Insights/Results:

Rate Yourself - Does this trade:

1. Follow system rules?

   1   2   3   4   5

2. Result in fear/anxiety? (If high, why?)

   1   2   3   4   5

3. Spark "greed" or pride?

   1   2   3   4   5

TRADE CHECKLIST & JOURNAL

Date:	Symbol:	Trade Type:

Is this a counter-trend trade? YES ☐ NO ☐ | Trigger:

+ Supporting Evidence +	- Opposing Evidence -

Heads Up:

Entry Plan		Exit Plan	
Entry Order Price:		Technical Stop:	
Max Stop Price:		Exit Target/Trigger:	
Size:		Time Stop:	
Max $ Loss		Est. Risk/Reward:	

Orders/Alerts Placed?   YES ☐   NO ☐ | Notes/Insights/Results:

Rate Yourself - Does this trade:

1. Follow system rules?
   1   2   3   4   5

2. Result in fear/anxiety? (If high, why?)
   1   2   3   4   5

3. Spark "greed" or pride?
   1   2   3   4   5

TRADE CHECKLIST & JOURNAL

Date:	Symbol:	Trade Type:

Is this a counter-trend trade? YES ☐ NO ☐

Trigger:

+ Supporting Evidence +	- Opposing Evidence -

Heads Up:

Entry Plan		Exit Plan	
Entry Order Price:		Technical Stop:	
Max Stop Price:		Exit Target/Trigger:	
Size:		Time Stop:	
Max $ Loss		Est. Risk/Reward:	

Orders/Alerts Placed?   YES ☐   NO ☐

Notes/Insights/Results:

Rate Yourself - Does this trade:

1. Follow system rules?

   1   2   3   4   5

2. Result in fear/anxiety? (If high, why?)

   1   2   3   4   5

3. Spark "greed" or pride?

   1   2   3   4   5

TRADE CHECKLIST & JOURNAL

Date:	Symbol:	Trade Type:

Is this a counter-trend trade?   YES ☐   NO ☐

Trigger:

+ Supporting Evidence +	- Opposing Evidence -

Heads Up:

Entry Plan		Exit Plan	
Entry Order Price:		Technical Stop:	
Max Stop Price:		Exit Target/Trigger:	
Size:		Time Stop:	
Max $ Loss		Est. Risk/Reward:	

Orders/Alerts Placed?   YES ☐   NO ☐

Notes/Insights/Results:

Rate Yourself - Does this trade:

1. Follow system rules?

   1   2   3   4   5

2. Result in fear/anxiety? (If high, why?)

   1   2   3   4   5

3. Spark "greed" or pride?

   1   2   3   4   5

TRADE CHECKLIST & JOURNAL

Date:	Symbol:	Trade Type:

Is this a counter-trend trade?   YES ☐   NO ☐   Trigger:

+ Supporting Evidence +	**- Opposing Evidence -**

Heads Up:

Entry Plan		**Exit Plan**	
Entry Order Price:		Technical Stop:	
Max Stop Price:		Exit Target/Trigger:	
Size:		Time Stop:	
Max $ Loss		Est. Risk/Reward:	

Orders/Alerts Placed?   YES ☐   NO ☐

Notes/Insights/Results:

Rate Yourself - Does this trade:

1. Follow system rules?

   1   2   3   4   5

2. Result in fear/anxiety? (If high, why?)

   1   2   3   4   5

3. Spark "greed" or pride?

   1   2   3   4   5

"Markets aren't chaotic, just as the seasons follow a series of predictable trends, so does price action. Stocks are like everything else in the world: they move in trends, and trends tend to persist."
JONATHAN HOENIG

TRADE CHECKLIST & JOURNAL

Date:	Symbol:	Trade Type:

Is this a counter-trend trade? YES ☐ NO ☐ | Trigger:

+ Supporting Evidence +	- Opposing Evidence -

Heads Up:

Entry Plan		Exit Plan	
Entry Order Price:		Technical Stop:	
Max Stop Price:		Exit Target/Trigger:	
Size:		Time Stop:	
Max $ Loss		Est. Risk/Reward:	

Orders/Alerts Placed?   YES ☐   NO ☐ | Notes/Insights/Results:

Rate Yourself - Does this trade:

1. Follow system rules?

   1   **2**   **3**   **4**   **5**

2. Result in fear/anxiety? (If high, why?)

   1   **2**   **3**   **4**   **5**

3. Spark "greed" or pride?

   1   **2**   **3**   **4**   **5**

TRADE CHECKLIST & JOURNAL

Date:	Symbol:	Trade Type:

Is this a counter-trend trade?   YES ☐   NO ☐ | Trigger:

+ Supporting Evidence +	- Opposing Evidence -

Heads Up:

Entry Plan		Exit Plan	
Entry Order Price:		Technical Stop:	
Max Stop Price:		Exit Target/Trigger:	
Size:		Time Stop:	
Max $ Loss		Est. Risk/Reward:	

Orders/Alerts Placed?   YES ☐   NO ☐ | Notes/Insights/Results:

Rate Yourself - Does this trade:

1. Follow system rules?

   1   2   3   4   5

2. Result in fear/anxiety? (If high, why?)

   1   2   3   4   5

3. Spark "greed" or pride?

   1   2   3   4   5

TRADE CHECKLIST & JOURNAL

Date:	Symbol:	Trade Type:

Is this a counter-trend trade?   YES ☐   NO ☐

Trigger:

+ Supporting Evidence +	- Opposing Evidence -

Heads Up:

Entry Plan		Exit Plan	
Entry Order Price:		Technical Stop:	
Max Stop Price:		Exit Target/Trigger:	
Size:		Time Stop:	
Max $ Loss		Est. Risk/Reward:	

Orders/Alerts Placed?   YES ☐   NO ☐

Notes/Insights/Results:

Rate Yourself - Does this trade:

1. Follow system rules?

   1   2   3   4   5

2. Result in fear/anxiety? (If high, why?)

   1   2   3   4   5

3. Spark "greed" or pride?

   1   2   3   4   5

TRADE CHECKLIST & JOURNAL

Date:	Symbol:	Trade Type:

Is this a counter-trend trade?   YES ☐   NO ☐   Trigger:

+ Supporting Evidence +	- Opposing Evidence -

Heads Up:

Entry Plan		Exit Plan	
Entry Order Price:		Technical Stop:	
Max Stop Price:		Exit Target/Trigger:	
Size:		Time Stop:	
Max $ Loss		Est. Risk/Reward:	

Orders/Alerts Placed?   YES ☐   NO ☐   Notes/Insights/Results:

Rate Yourself - Does this trade:

1. Follow system rules?
   1   2   3   4   5

2. Result in fear/anxiety? (If high, why?)
   1   2   3   4   5

3. Spark "greed" or pride?
   1   2   3   4   5

TRADE CHECKLIST & JOURNAL

Date:	Symbol:	Trade Type:

Is this a counter-trend trade? YES ☐ NO ☐

Trigger:

+ Supporting Evidence +	- Opposing Evidence -

Heads Up:

Entry Plan		Exit Plan	
Entry Order Price:		Technical Stop:	
Max Stop Price:		Exit Target/Trigger:	
Size:		Time Stop:	
Max $ Loss		Est. Risk/Reward:	

Orders/Alerts Placed?   YES ☐   NO ☐

Notes/Insights/Results:

Rate Yourself - Does this trade:

1. Follow system rules?

   1   2   3   4   5

2. Result in fear/anxiety? (If high, why?)

   1   2   3   4   5

3. Spark "greed" or pride?

   1   2   3   4   5

TRADE CHECKLIST & JOURNAL

Date:	Symbol:	Trade Type:

Is this a counter-trend trade?   YES ☐   NO ☐ | Trigger:

+ Supporting Evidence +	**- Opposing Evidence -**

Heads Up:

Entry Plan		**Exit Plan**	
Entry Order Price:		Technical Stop:	
Max Stop Price:		Exit Target/Trigger:	
Size:		Time Stop:	
Max $ Loss		Est. Risk/Reward:	

Orders/Alerts Placed?   YES ☐   NO ☐ | Notes/Insights/Results:

Rate Yourself - Does this trade:

1. Follow system rules?

   1   2   3   4   5

2. Result in fear/anxiety? (If high, why?)

   1   2   3   4   5

3. Spark "greed" or pride?

   1   2   3   4   5

TRADE CHECKLIST & JOURNAL

Date:	Symbol:	Trade Type:

Is this a counter-trend trade?   YES ☐   NO ☐

Trigger:

+ Supporting Evidence +	- Opposing Evidence -

Heads Up:

Entry Plan		Exit Plan	
Entry Order Price:		Technical Stop:	
Max Stop Price:		Exit Target/Trigger:	
Size:		Time Stop:	
Max $ Loss		Est. Risk/Reward:	

Orders/Alerts Placed?   YES ☐   NO ☐

Notes/Insights/Results:

Rate Yourself - Does this trade:

1. Follow system rules?

   1   2   3   4   5

2. Result in fear/anxiety? (If high, why?)

   1   2   3   4   5

3. Spark "greed" or pride?

   1   2   3   4   5

TRADE CHECKLIST & JOURNAL

Date:	Symbol:	Trade Type:

Is this a counter-trend trade?   YES ☐   NO ☐

Trigger:

+ Supporting Evidence +	- Opposing Evidence -

Heads Up:

Entry Plan		Exit Plan	
Entry Order Price:		Technical Stop:	
Max Stop Price:		Exit Target/Trigger:	
Size:		Time Stop:	
Max $ Loss		Est. Risk/Reward:	

Orders/Alerts Placed?   YES ☐   NO ☐

Notes/Insights/Results:

Rate Yourself - Does this trade:

1. Follow system rules?

   1   2   3   4   5

2. Result in fear/anxiety? (If high, why?)

   1   2   3   4   5

3. Spark "greed" or pride?

   1   2   3   4   5

TRADE CHECKLIST & JOURNAL

Date:	Symbol:	Trade Type:

Is this a counter-trend trade?   YES ☐   NO ☐ | Trigger: |

+ Supporting Evidence +	- Opposing Evidence -

Heads Up:

Entry Plan		Exit Plan	
Entry Order Price:		Technical Stop:	
Max Stop Price:		Exit Target/Trigger:	
Size:		Time Stop:	
Max $ Loss		Est. Risk/Reward:	

Orders/Alerts Placed?   YES ☐   NO ☐   Notes/Insights/Results:

Rate Yourself - Does this trade:

1. Follow system rules?
   1   2   3   4   5

2. Result in fear/anxiety? (If high, why?)
   1   2   3   4   5

3. Spark "greed" or pride?
   1   2   3   4   5

TRADE CHECKLIST & JOURNAL

Date:	Symbol:	Trade Type:

Is this a counter-trend trade?   YES ☐   NO ☐ | Trigger:

+ Supporting Evidence +	- Opposing Evidence -

Heads Up:

Entry Plan		Exit Plan	
Entry Order Price:		Technical Stop:	
Max Stop Price:		Exit Target/Trigger:	
Size:		Time Stop:	
Max $ Loss		Est. Risk/Reward:	

Orders/Alerts Placed?   YES ☐   NO ☐   Notes/Insights/Results:

Rate Yourself - Does this trade:

1. Follow system rules?

    1   2   3   4   5

2. Result in fear/anxiety? (If high, why?)

    1   2   3   4   5

3. Spark "greed" or pride?

    1   2   3   4   5

"Quality of belief determines quality of action—
faulty beliefs lead to faulty actions!"
DENNIS WILBORN

TRADE CHECKLIST & JOURNAL

Date:	Symbol:	Trade Type:

Is this a counter-trend trade?   YES ☐   NO ☐ | Trigger:

+ Supporting Evidence +	- Opposing Evidence -

Heads Up:

Entry Plan		Exit Plan	
Entry Order Price:		Technical Stop:	
Max Stop Price:		Exit Target/Trigger:	
Size:		Time Stop:	
Max $ Loss		Est. Risk/Reward:	

Orders/Alerts Placed?   YES ☐   NO ☐   Notes/Insights/Results:

Rate Yourself - Does this trade:

1. Follow system rules?

   1   2   3   4   5

2. Result in fear/anxiety? (If high, why?)

   1   2   3   4   5

3. Spark "greed" or pride?

   1   2   3   4   5

TRADE CHECKLIST & JOURNAL

Date:	Symbol:	Trade Type:

Is this a counter-trend trade?   YES ☐   NO ☐ | Trigger:

+ Supporting Evidence +	- Opposing Evidence -

Heads Up:

Entry Plan		Exit Plan	
Entry Order Price:		Technical Stop:	
Max Stop Price:		Exit Target/Trigger:	
Size:		Time Stop:	
Max $ Loss		Est. Risk/Reward:	

Orders/Alerts Placed?   YES ☐   NO ☐ | Notes/Insights/Results:

Rate Yourself - Does this trade:

1. Follow system rules?

    1   2   3   4   5

2. Result in fear/anxiety? (If high, why?)

    1   2   3   4   5

3. Spark "greed" or pride?

    1   2   3   4   5

TRADE CHECKLIST & JOURNAL

Date:	Symbol:	Trade Type:

Is this a counter-trend trade?   YES ☐   NO ☐

Trigger:

+ Supporting Evidence +	**- Opposing Evidence -**

Heads Up:

Entry Plan		**Exit Plan**	
Entry Order Price:		Technical Stop:	
Max Stop Price:		Exit Target/Trigger:	
Size:		Time Stop:	
Max $ Loss		Est. Risk/Reward:	

Orders/Alerts Placed?   YES ☐   NO ☐

Notes/Insights/Results:

Rate Yourself - Does this trade:

1. Follow system rules?

   1   2   3   4   5

2. Result in fear/anxiety? (If high, why?)

   1   2   3   4   5

3. Spark "greed" or pride?

   1   2   3   4   5

TRADE CHECKLIST & JOURNAL

Date:	Symbol:	Trade Type:

Is this a counter-trend trade?   YES ☐   NO ☐ | Trigger:

+ Supporting Evidence +	- Opposing Evidence -

Heads Up:

Entry Plan		Exit Plan	
Entry Order Price:		Technical Stop:	
Max Stop Price:		Exit Target/Trigger:	
Size:		Time Stop:	
Max $ Loss		Est. Risk/Reward:	

Orders/Alerts Placed?   YES ☐   NO ☐

Rate Yourself - Does this trade:

1. Follow system rules?

   1   2   3   4   5

2. Result in fear/anxiety? (If high, why?)

   1   2   3   4   5

3. Spark "greed" or pride?

   1   2   3   4   5

Notes/Insights/Results:

TRADE CHECKLIST & JOURNAL

Date:	Symbol:	Trade Type:

Is this a counter-trend trade? YES ☐ NO ☐ | Trigger:

+ Supporting Evidence +	- Opposing Evidence -

Heads Up:

Entry Plan		Exit Plan	
Entry Order Price:		Technical Stop:	
Max Stop Price:		Exit Target/Trigger:	
Size:		Time Stop:	
Max $ Loss		Est. Risk/Reward:	

Orders/Alerts Placed? YES ☐ NO ☐   Notes/Insights/Results:

Rate Yourself - Does this trade:

1. Follow system rules?

   1   2   3   4   5

2. Result in fear/anxiety? (If high, why?)

   1   2   3   4   5

3. Spark "greed" or pride?

   1   2   3   4   5

TRADE CHECKLIST & JOURNAL

Date:	Symbol:	Trade Type:

Is this a counter-trend trade? YES ☐   NO ☐ | Trigger:

+ Supporting Evidence +	- Opposing Evidence -

Heads Up:

Entry Plan		Exit Plan	
Entry Order Price:		Technical Stop:	
Max Stop Price:		Exit Target/Trigger:	
Size:		Time Stop:	
Max $ Loss		Est. Risk/Reward:	

Orders/Alerts Placed?   YES ☐   NO ☐ | Notes/Insights/Results:

Rate Yourself - Does this trade:

1. Follow system rules?

   1   2   3   4   5

2. Result in fear/anxiety? (If high, why?)

   1   2   3   4   5

3. Spark "greed" or pride?

   1   2   3   4   5

TRADE CHECKLIST & JOURNAL

Date:	Symbol:	Trade Type:

Is this a counter-trend trade?   YES ☐   NO ☐ | Trigger:

+ Supporting Evidence +	- Opposing Evidence -

Heads Up:

Entry Plan		Exit Plan	
Entry Order Price:		Technical Stop:	
Max Stop Price:		Exit Target/Trigger:	
Size:		Time Stop:	
Max $ Loss		Est. Risk/Reward:	

Orders/Alerts Placed?   YES ☐   NO ☐   Notes/Insights/Results:

Rate Yourself - Does this trade:

1. Follow system rules?

   1   2   3   4   5

2. Result in fear/anxiety? (If high, why?)

   1   2   3   4   5

3. Spark "greed" or pride?

   1   2   3   4   5

TRADE CHECKLIST & JOURNAL

Date:	Symbol:	Trade Type:

Is this a counter-trend trade?   YES ☐   NO ☐ | Trigger:

+ Supporting Evidence +	- Opposing Evidence -

Heads Up:

Entry Plan		Exit Plan	
Entry Order Price:		Technical Stop:	
Max Stop Price:		Exit Target/Trigger:	
Size:		Time Stop:	
Max $ Loss		Est. Risk/Reward:	

Orders/Alerts Placed?   YES ☐   NO ☐ | Notes/Insights/Results:

Rate Yourself - Does this trade:

1. Follow system rules?

   1   2   3   4   5

2. Result in fear/anxiety? (If high, why?)

   1   2   3   4   5

3. Spark "greed" or pride?

   1   2   3   4   5

TRADE CHECKLIST & JOURNAL

Date:	Symbol:	Trade Type:

Is this a counter-trend trade?   YES ☐   NO ☐ | Trigger:

+ Supporting Evidence +	- Opposing Evidence -

Heads Up:

Entry Plan		Exit Plan	
Entry Order Price:		Technical Stop:	
Max Stop Price:		Exit Target/Trigger:	
Size:		Time Stop:	
Max $ Loss		Est. Risk/Reward:	

Orders/Alerts Placed?   YES ☐   NO ☐

Notes/Insights/Results:

Rate Yourself - Does this trade:

1. Follow system rules?

   1   2   3   4   5

2. Result in fear/anxiety? (If high, why?)

   1   2   3   4   5

3. Spark "greed" or pride?

   1   2   3   4   5

TRADE CHECKLIST & JOURNAL

Date:	Symbol:	Trade Type:

Is this a counter-trend trade? YES ☐ NO ☐ | Trigger:

+ Supporting Evidence +	- Opposing Evidence -

Heads Up:

Entry Plan		Exit Plan	
Entry Order Price:		Technical Stop:	
Max Stop Price:		Exit Target/Trigger:	
Size:		Time Stop:	
Max $ Loss		Est. Risk/Reward:	

Orders/Alerts Placed? YES ☐ NO ☐

Notes/Insights/Results:

Rate Yourself - Does this trade:

1. Follow system rules?

   1   2   3   4   5

2. Result in fear/anxiety? (If high, why?)

   1   2   3   4   5

3. Spark "greed" or pride?

   1   2   3   4   5

"Money management is the true survival key."
BILL DUNN

TRADE CHECKLIST & JOURNAL

Date:	Symbol:	Trade Type:

Is this a counter-trend trade? YES ☐ NO ☐ | Trigger:

+ Supporting Evidence +	- Opposing Evidence -

Heads Up:

Entry Plan		Exit Plan	
Entry Order Price:		Technical Stop:	
Max Stop Price:		Exit Target/Trigger:	
Size:		Time Stop:	
Max $ Loss		Est. Risk/Reward:	

Orders/Alerts Placed?   YES ☐   NO ☐   Notes/Insights/Results:

Rate Yourself - Does this trade:

1. Follow system rules?

    1   2   3   4   5

2. Result in fear/anxiety? (If high, why?)

    1   2   3   4   5

3. Spark "greed" or pride?

    1   2   3   4   5

TRADE CHECKLIST & JOURNAL

Date:	Symbol:	Trade Type:

Is this a counter-trend trade?   YES ☐   NO ☐ | Trigger:

+ Supporting Evidence +	- Opposing Evidence -

Heads Up:

Entry Plan		Exit Plan	
Entry Order Price:		Technical Stop:	
Max Stop Price:		Exit Target/Trigger:	
Size:		Time Stop:	
Max $ Loss		Est. Risk/Reward:	

Orders/Alerts Placed?   YES ☐   NO ☐   Notes/Insights/Results:

Rate Yourself - Does this trade:

1. Follow system rules?

   1   2   3   4   5

2. Result in fear/anxiety? (If high, why?)

   1   2   3   4   5

3. Spark "greed" or pride?

   1   2   3   4   5

TRADE CHECKLIST & JOURNAL

Date:	Symbol:	Trade Type:

Is this a counter-trend trade?   YES ☐   NO ☐

Trigger:

+ Supporting Evidence +	- Opposing Evidence -

Heads Up:

Entry Plan		Exit Plan	
Entry Order Price:		Technical Stop:	
Max Stop Price:		Exit Target/Trigger:	
Size:		Time Stop:	
Max $ Loss		Est. Risk/Reward:	

Orders/Alerts Placed?   YES ☐   NO ☐

Notes/Insights/Results:

Rate Yourself - Does this trade:

1. Follow system rules?

   1   2   3   4   5

2. Result in fear/anxiety? (If high, why?)

   1   2   3   4   5

3. Spark "greed" or pride?

   1   2   3   4   5

TRADE CHECKLIST & JOURNAL

Date:	Symbol:	Trade Type:

Is this a counter-trend trade?   YES ☐   NO ☐ | Trigger:

+ Supporting Evidence +	- Opposing Evidence -

Heads Up:

Entry Plan		Exit Plan	
Entry Order Price:		Technical Stop:	
Max Stop Price:		Exit Target/Trigger:	
Size:		Time Stop:	
Max $ Loss		Est. Risk/Reward:	

Orders/Alerts Placed?   YES ☐   NO ☐

Notes/Insights/Results:

Rate Yourself - Does this trade:

1. Follow system rules?
   1   2   3   4   5

2. Result in fear/anxiety? (If high, why?)
   1   2   3   4   5

3. Spark "greed" or pride?
   1   2   3   4   5

TRADE CHECKLIST & JOURNAL

Date:	Symbol:	Trade Type:

Is this a counter-trend trade?   YES ☐   NO ☐

Trigger:

+ Supporting Evidence +	**– Opposing Evidence –**

Heads Up:

Entry Plan		**Exit Plan**	
Entry Order Price:		Technical Stop:	
Max Stop Price:		Exit Target/Trigger:	
Size:		Time Stop:	
Max $ Loss		Est. Risk/Reward:	

Orders/Alerts Placed?   YES ☐   NO ☐

Notes/Insights/Results:

Rate Yourself - Does this trade:

1. Follow system rules?

    1   2   3   4   5

2. Result in fear/anxiety? (If high, why?)

    1   2   3   4   5

3. Spark "greed" or pride?

    1   2   3   4   5

TRADE CHECKLIST & JOURNAL

Date:	Symbol:	Trade Type:

Is this a counter-trend trade? YES ☐ NO ☐ | Trigger:

+ Supporting Evidence +	- Opposing Evidence -

Heads Up:

Entry Plan		Exit Plan	
Entry Order Price:		Technical Stop:	
Max Stop Price:		Exit Target/Trigger:	
Size:		Time Stop:	
Max $ Loss		Est. Risk/Reward:	

Orders/Alerts Placed?   YES ☐   NO ☐ | Notes/Insights/Results:

Rate Yourself - Does this trade:

1. Follow system rules?
   1   2   3   4   5

2. Result in fear/anxiety? (If high, why?)
   1   2   3   4   5

3. Spark "greed" or pride?
   1   2   3   4   5

TRADE CHECKLIST & JOURNAL

Date:	Symbol:	Trade Type:

Is this a counter-trend trade? YES ☐ NO ☐ | Trigger: |

+ Supporting Evidence +	**- Opposing Evidence -**

Heads Up:

Entry Plan		**Exit Plan**	
Entry Order Price:		Technical Stop:	
Max Stop Price:		Exit Target/Trigger:	
Size:		Time Stop:	
Max $ Loss		Est. Risk/Reward:	

Orders/Alerts Placed?   YES ☐   NO ☐ | Notes/Insights/Results:

Rate Yourself - Does this trade:

1. Follow system rules?

   1   2   3   4   5

2. Result in fear/anxiety? (If high, why?)

   1   2   3   4   5

3. Spark "greed" or pride?

   1   2   3   4   5

TRADE CHECKLIST & JOURNAL

Date:	Symbol:	Trade Type:

Is this a counter-trend trade?   YES ☐   NO ☐ | Trigger:

+ Supporting Evidence +	- Opposing Evidence -

Heads Up:

Entry Plan		Exit Plan	
Entry Order Price:		Technical Stop:	
Max Stop Price:		Exit Target/Trigger:	
Size:		Time Stop:	
Max $ Loss		Est. Risk/Reward:	

Orders/Alerts Placed?   YES ☐   NO ☐ | Notes/Insights/Results:

Rate Yourself - Does this trade:

1. Follow system rules?

   1   2   3   4   5

2. Result in fear/anxiety? (If high, why?)

   1   2   3   4   5

3. Spark "greed" or pride?

   1   2   3   4   5

TRADE CHECKLIST & JOURNAL

Date:	Symbol:	Trade Type:

Is this a counter-trend trade?   YES ☐   NO ☐   Trigger:

+ Supporting Evidence +	- Opposing Evidence -

Heads Up:

Entry Plan		Exit Plan	
Entry Order Price:		Technical Stop:	
Max Stop Price:		Exit Target/Trigger:	
Size:		Time Stop:	
Max $ Loss		Est. Risk/Reward:	

Orders/Alerts Placed?   YES ☐   NO ☐   Notes/Insights/Results:

Rate Yourself - Does this trade:

1. Follow system rules?

   1   2   3   4   5

2. Result in fear/anxiety? (If high, why?)

   1   2   3   4   5

3. Spark "greed" or pride?

   1   2   3   4   5

TRADE CHECKLIST & JOURNAL

Date:	Symbol:	Trade Type:

Is this a counter-trend trade?   YES ☐   NO ☐ | Trigger:

+ Supporting Evidence +	**- Opposing Evidence -**

Heads Up:

Entry Plan		**Exit Plan**	
Entry Order Price:		Technical Stop:	
Max Stop Price:		Exit Target/Trigger:	
Size:		Time Stop:	
Max $ Loss		Est. Risk/Reward:	

Orders/Alerts Placed?   YES ☐   NO ☐   Notes/Insights/Results:

Rate Yourself - Does this trade:

1. Follow system rules?

   1   2   3   4   5

2. Result in fear/anxiety? (If high, why?)

   1   2   3   4   5

3. Spark "greed" or pride?

   1   2   3   4   5

"Compound interest is the 8th wonder of the world. He who understands it earns it; he who doesn't, pays it."

ALBERT EINSTEIN

TRADE CHECKLIST & JOURNAL

Date:	Symbol:	Trade Type:

Is this a counter-trend trade?   YES ☐   NO ☐   Trigger:

+ Supporting Evidence +	- Opposing Evidence -

Heads Up:

Entry Plan		Exit Plan	
Entry Order Price:		Technical Stop:	
Max Stop Price:		Exit Target/Trigger:	
Size:		Time Stop:	
Max $ Loss		Est. Risk/Reward:	

Orders/Alerts Placed?   YES ☐   NO ☐   Notes/Insights/Results:

Rate Yourself - Does this trade:

1. Follow system rules?

      1   **2**   **3**   **4**   **5**

2. Result in fear/anxiety? (If high, why?)

      1   **2**   **3**   **4**   **5**

3. Spark "greed" or pride?

      1   **2**   **3**   **4**   **5**

TRADE CHECKLIST & JOURNAL

Date:	Symbol:	Trade Type:

Is this a counter-trend trade?　YES ☐　NO ☐　| Trigger:

+ Supporting Evidence +	- Opposing Evidence -

Heads Up:

Entry Plan		Exit Plan	
Entry Order Price:		Technical Stop:	
Max Stop Price:		Exit Target/Trigger:	
Size:		Time Stop:	
Max $ Loss		Est. Risk/Reward:	

Orders/Alerts Placed?　YES ☐　NO ☐

Rate Yourself - Does this trade:

1. Follow system rules?

   1　　2　　3　　4　　5

2. Result in fear/anxiety? (If high, why?)

   1　　2　　3　　4　　5

3. Spark "greed" or pride?

   1　　2　　3　　4　　5

Notes/Insights/Results:

TRADE CHECKLIST & JOURNAL

Date:	Symbol:	Trade Type:

Is this a counter-trend trade?   YES ☐   NO ☐ | Trigger:

+ Supporting Evidence +	- Opposing Evidence -

Heads Up:

Entry Plan		Exit Plan	
Entry Order Price:		Technical Stop:	
Max Stop Price:		Exit Target/Trigger:	
Size:		Time Stop:	
Max $ Loss		Est. Risk/Reward:	

Orders/Alerts Placed?   YES ☐   NO ☐ | Notes/Insights/Results:

Rate Yourself - Does this trade:

1. Follow system rules?
   1   2   3   4   5

2. Result in fear/anxiety? (If high, why?)
   1   2   3   4   5

3. Spark "greed" or pride?
   1   2   3   4   5

TRADE CHECKLIST & JOURNAL

Date:	Symbol:	Trade Type:

Is this a counter-trend trade? YES ☐ NO ☐

Trigger:

+ Supporting Evidence +	- Opposing Evidence -

Heads Up:

Entry Plan		Exit Plan	
Entry Order Price:		Technical Stop:	
Max Stop Price:		Exit Target/Trigger:	
Size:		Time Stop:	
Max $ Loss		Est. Risk/Reward:	

Orders/Alerts Placed? YES ☐ NO ☐

Notes/Insights/Results:

Rate Yourself - Does this trade:

1. Follow system rules?

   1   2   3   4   5

2. Result in fear/anxiety? (If high, why?)

   1   2   3   4   5

3. Spark "greed" or pride?

   1   2   3   4   5

TRADE CHECKLIST & JOURNAL

Date:	Symbol:	Trade Type:

Is this a counter-trend trade?   YES ☐   NO ☐ | Trigger:

+ Supporting Evidence +	- Opposing Evidence -

Heads Up:

Entry Plan		Exit Plan	
Entry Order Price:		Technical Stop:	
Max Stop Price:		Exit Target/Trigger:	
Size:		Time Stop:	
Max $ Loss		Est. Risk/Reward:	

Orders/Alerts Placed?   YES ☐   NO ☐ | Notes/Insights/Results:

Rate Yourself - Does this trade:

1. Follow system rules?
   1   2   3   4   5

2. Result in fear/anxiety? (If high, why?)
   1   2   3   4   5

3. Spark "greed" or pride?
   1   2   3   4   5

TRADE CHECKLIST & JOURNAL

Date:	Symbol:	Trade Type:

Is this a counter-trend trade?   YES ☐   NO ☐ | Trigger:

+ Supporting Evidence +	- Opposing Evidence -

Heads Up:

Entry Plan		Exit Plan	
Entry Order Price:		Technical Stop:	
Max Stop Price:		Exit Target/Trigger:	
Size:		Time Stop:	
Max $ Loss		Est. Risk/Reward:	

Orders/Alerts Placed?   YES ☐   NO ☐ | Notes/Insights/Results:

Rate Yourself - Does this trade:

1. Follow system rules?

   1   2   3   4   5

2. Result in fear/anxiety? (If high, why?)

   1   2   3   4   5

3. Spark "greed" or pride?

   1   2   3   4   5

TRADE CHECKLIST & JOURNAL

Date:	Symbol:	Trade Type:

Is this a counter-trend trade?   YES ☐   NO ☐ | Trigger:

+ Supporting Evidence +	- Opposing Evidence -

Heads Up:

Entry Plan		Exit Plan	
Entry Order Price:		Technical Stop:	
Max Stop Price:		Exit Target/Trigger:	
Size:		Time Stop:	
Max $ Loss		Est. Risk/Reward:	

Orders/Alerts Placed?   YES ☐   NO ☐   Notes/Insights/Results:

Rate Yourself - Does this trade:

1. Follow system rules?

   1   2   3   4   5

2. Result in fear/anxiety? (If high, why?)

   1   2   3   4   5

3. Spark "greed" or pride?

   1   2   3   4   5

TRADE CHECKLIST & JOURNAL

Date:	Symbol:	Trade Type:

Is this a counter-trend trade?   YES ☐   NO ☐

Trigger:

+ Supporting Evidence +	- Opposing Evidence -

Heads Up:

Entry Plan		Exit Plan	
Entry Order Price:		Technical Stop:	
Max Stop Price:		Exit Target/Trigger:	
Size:		Time Stop:	
Max $ Loss		Est. Risk/Reward:	

Orders/Alerts Placed?   YES ☐   NO ☐

Notes/Insights/Results:

Rate Yourself - Does this trade:

1. Follow system rules?

    1   2   3   4   5

2. Result in fear/anxiety? (If high, why?)

    1   2   3   4   5

3. Spark "greed" or pride?

    1   2   3   4   5

TRADE CHECKLIST & JOURNAL

Date:	Symbol:	Trade Type:

Is this a counter-trend trade?   YES ☐   NO ☐ | Trigger: |

+ Supporting Evidence +	- Opposing Evidence -

Heads Up:

Entry Plan		Exit Plan	
Entry Order Price:		Technical Stop:	
Max Stop Price:		Exit Target/Trigger:	
Size:		Time Stop:	
Max $ Loss		Est. Risk/Reward:	

Orders/Alerts Placed?   YES ☐   NO ☐   Notes/Insights/Results:

Rate Yourself - Does this trade:

1. Follow system rules?

   1   2   3   4   5

2. Result in fear/anxiety? (If high, why?)

   1   2   3   4   5

3. Spark "greed" or pride?

   1   2   3   4   5

TRADE CHECKLIST & JOURNAL

Date:	Symbol:	Trade Type:

Is this a counter-trend trade?   YES ☐   NO ☐ | Trigger:

+ Supporting Evidence +	**- Opposing Evidence -**

Heads Up:

Entry Plan		**Exit Plan**	
Entry Order Price:		Technical Stop:	
Max Stop Price:		Exit Target/Trigger:	
Size:		Time Stop:	
Max $ Loss		Est. Risk/Reward:	

Orders/Alerts Placed?   YES ☐   NO ☐ | Notes/Insights/Results:

Rate Yourself - Does this trade:

1. Follow system rules?

   1   2   3   4   5

2. Result in fear/anxiety? (If high, why?)

   1   2   3   4   5

3. Spark "greed" or pride?

   1   2   3   4   5

"A trend should be assumed to continue in effect until such time as its reversal has been definitely signaled."

EDWARDS & MAGEE

TRADE CHECKLIST & JOURNAL

Date:	Symbol:	Trade Type:

Is this a counter-trend trade?   YES ☐   NO ☐

Trigger:

+ Supporting Evidence +	- Opposing Evidence -

Heads Up:

Entry Plan		Exit Plan	
Entry Order Price:		Technical Stop:	
Max Stop Price:		Exit Target/Trigger:	
Size:		Time Stop:	
Max $ Loss		Est. Risk/Reward:	

Orders/Alerts Placed?   YES ☐   NO ☐

Notes/Insights/Results:

Rate Yourself - Does this trade:

1. Follow system rules?

   1   2   3   4   5

2. Result in fear/anxiety? (If high, why?)

   1   2   3   4   5

3. Spark "greed" or pride?

   1   2   3   4   5

TRADE CHECKLIST & JOURNAL

Date:	Symbol:	Trade Type:

Is this a counter-trend trade?   YES ☐   NO ☐   Trigger:

+ Supporting Evidence +	- Opposing Evidence -

Heads Up:

Entry Plan		Exit Plan	
Entry Order Price:		Technical Stop:	
Max Stop Price:		Exit Target/Trigger:	
Size:		Time Stop:	
Max $ Loss		Est. Risk/Reward:	

Orders/Alerts Placed?   YES ☐   NO ☐   Notes/Insights/Results:

Rate Yourself - Does this trade:

1. Follow system rules?

   1   2   3   4   5

2. Result in fear/anxiety? (If high, why?)

   1   2   3   4   5

3. Spark "greed" or pride?

   1   2   3   4   5

TRADE CHECKLIST & JOURNAL

Date:	Symbol:	Trade Type:

Is this a counter-trend trade?   YES ☐   NO ☐   Trigger:

+ Supporting Evidence +	- Opposing Evidence -

Heads Up:

Entry Plan		Exit Plan	
Entry Order Price:		Technical Stop:	
Max Stop Price:		Exit Target/Trigger:	
Size:		Time Stop:	
Max $ Loss		Est. Risk/Reward:	

Orders/Alerts Placed?   YES ☐   NO ☐

Notes/Insights/Results:

Rate Yourself - Does this trade:

1. Follow system rules?

   1   2   3   4   5

2. Result in fear/anxiety? (If high, why?)

   1   2   3   4   5

3. Spark "greed" or pride?

   1   2   3   4   5

TRADE CHECKLIST & JOURNAL

Date:	Symbol:	Trade Type:

Is this a counter-trend trade? YES ☐ NO ☐   Trigger:

+ Supporting Evidence +	- Opposing Evidence -

Heads Up:

Entry Plan		Exit Plan	
Entry Order Price:		Technical Stop:	
Max Stop Price:		Exit Target/Trigger:	
Size:		Time Stop:	
Max $ Loss		Est. Risk/Reward:	

Orders/Alerts Placed?   YES ☐   NO ☐   Notes/Insights/Results:

Rate Yourself - Does this trade:

1. Follow system rules?

   1   2   3   4   5

2. Result in fear/anxiety? (If high, why?)

   1   2   3   4   5

3. Spark "greed" or pride?

   1   2   3   4   5

TRADE CHECKLIST & JOURNAL

Date:	Symbol:	Trade Type:

Is this a counter-trend trade?   YES ☐   NO ☐ | Trigger:

+ Supporting Evidence +	- Opposing Evidence -

Heads Up:

Entry Plan		Exit Plan	
Entry Order Price:		Technical Stop:	
Max Stop Price:		Exit Target/Trigger:	
Size:		Time Stop:	
Max $ Loss		Est. Risk/Reward:	

Orders/Alerts Placed?   YES ☐   NO ☐ | Notes/Insights/Results:

Rate Yourself - Does this trade:

1. Follow system rules?

   1   2   3   4   5

2. Result in fear/anxiety? (If high, why?)

   1   2   3   4   5

3. Spark "greed" or pride?

   1   2   3   4   5

TRADE CHECKLIST & JOURNAL

Date:	Symbol:	Trade Type:

Is this a counter-trend trade?   YES ☐   NO ☐ | Trigger:

+ Supporting Evidence +	- Opposing Evidence -

Heads Up:

Entry Plan		Exit Plan	
Entry Order Price:		Technical Stop:	
Max Stop Price:		Exit Target/Trigger:	
Size:		Time Stop:	
Max $ Loss		Est. Risk/Reward:	

Orders/Alerts Placed?   YES ☐   NO ☐   Notes/Insights/Results:

Rate Yourself - Does this trade:

1. Follow system rules?

   1   2   3   4   5

2. Result in fear/anxiety? (If high, why?)

   1   2   3   4   5

3. Spark "greed" or pride?

   1   2   3   4   5

TRADE CHECKLIST & JOURNAL

Date:	Symbol:	Trade Type:

Is this a counter-trend trade?   YES ☐   NO ☐ | Trigger:

+ Supporting Evidence +	- Opposing Evidence -

Heads Up:

Entry Plan		Exit Plan	
Entry Order Price:		Technical Stop:	
Max Stop Price:		Exit Target/Trigger:	
Size:		Time Stop:	
Max $ Loss		Est. Risk/Reward:	

Orders/Alerts Placed?   YES ☐   NO ☐

Rate Yourself - Does this trade:

1. Follow system rules?

   1   2   3   4   5

2. Result in fear/anxiety? (If high, why?)

   1   2   3   4   5

3. Spark "greed" or pride?

   1   2   3   4   5

Notes/Insights/Results:

TRADE CHECKLIST & JOURNAL

Date:	Symbol:	Trade Type:

Is this a counter-trend trade? YES ☐ NO ☐   Trigger:

+ Supporting Evidence +	- Opposing Evidence -

Heads Up:

Entry Plan		Exit Plan	
Entry Order Price:		Technical Stop:	
Max Stop Price:		Exit Target/Trigger:	
Size:		Time Stop:	
Max $ Loss		Est. Risk/Reward:	

Orders/Alerts Placed?   YES ☐   NO ☐

Notes/Insights/Results:

Rate Yourself - Does this trade:

1. Follow system rules?
   1   2   3   4   5

2. Result in fear/anxiety? (If high, why?)
   1   2   3   4   5

3. Spark "greed" or pride?
   1   2   3   4   5

TRADE CHECKLIST & JOURNAL

Date:	Symbol:	Trade Type:

Is this a counter-trend trade? YES ☐ NO ☐ | Trigger:

+ Supporting Evidence +	- Opposing Evidence -

Heads Up:

Entry Plan		Exit Plan	
Entry Order Price:		Technical Stop:	
Max Stop Price:		Exit Target/Trigger:	
Size:		Time Stop:	
Max $ Loss		Est. Risk/Reward:	

Orders/Alerts Placed?   YES ☐   NO ☐ | Notes/Insights/Results:

Rate Yourself - Does this trade:

1. Follow system rules?

   1   2   3   4   5

2. Result in fear/anxiety? (If high, why?)

   1   2   3   4   5

3. Spark "greed" or pride?

   1   2   3   4   5

TRADE CHECKLIST & JOURNAL

Date:	Symbol:	Trade Type:

Is this a counter-trend trade?   YES ☐   NO ☐ | Trigger:

+ Supporting Evidence +	- Opposing Evidence -

Heads Up:

Entry Plan		Exit Plan	
Entry Order Price:		Technical Stop:	
Max Stop Price:		Exit Target/Trigger:	
Size:		Time Stop:	
Max $ Loss		Est. Risk/Reward:	

Orders/Alerts Placed?   YES ☐   NO ☐

Notes/Insights/Results:

Rate Yourself - Does this trade:

1. Follow system rules?

   1   2   3   4   5

2. Result in fear/anxiety? (If high, why?)

   1   2   3   4   5

3. Spark "greed" or pride?

   1   2   3   4   5

"The difference between a successful person and others is not a lack of strength, not a lack of knowledge, but rather a lack of will."
VINCE LOMBARDI

TRADE CHECKLIST & JOURNAL

Date:	Symbol:	Trade Type:

Is this a counter-trend trade?   YES ☐   NO ☐ | Trigger:

+ Supporting Evidence +	- Opposing Evidence -

Heads Up:

Entry Plan		**Exit Plan**	
Entry Order Price:		Technical Stop:	
Max Stop Price:		Exit Target/Trigger:	
Size:		Time Stop:	
Max $ Loss		Est. Risk/Reward:	

Orders/Alerts Placed?   YES ☐   NO ☐   Notes/Insights/Results:

Rate Yourself - Does this trade:

1. Follow system rules?

   1   2   3   4   5

2. Result in fear/anxiety? (If high, why?)

   1   2   3   4   5

3. Spark "greed" or pride?

   1   2   3   4   5

TRADE CHECKLIST & JOURNAL

Date:	Symbol:	Trade Type:

Is this a counter-trend trade?   YES ☐   NO ☐

Trigger:

+ Supporting Evidence +	- Opposing Evidence -

Heads Up:

Entry Plan		Exit Plan	
Entry Order Price:		Technical Stop:	
Max Stop Price:		Exit Target/Trigger:	
Size:		Time Stop:	
Max $ Loss		Est. Risk/Reward:	

Orders/Alerts Placed?   YES ☐   NO ☐

Notes/Insights/Results:

Rate Yourself - Does this trade:

1. Follow system rules?

   1   2   3   4   5

2. Result in fear/anxiety? (If high, why?)

   1   2   3   4   5

3. Spark "greed" or pride?

   1   2   3   4   5

TRADE CHECKLIST & JOURNAL

Date:	Symbol:	Trade Type:

Is this a counter-trend trade?   YES ☐   NO ☐ | Trigger:

+ Supporting Evidence +	- Opposing Evidence -

Heads Up:

Entry Plan		Exit Plan	
Entry Order Price:		Technical Stop:	
Max Stop Price:		Exit Target/Trigger:	
Size:		Time Stop:	
Max $ Loss		Est. Risk/Reward:	

Orders/Alerts Placed?   YES ☐   NO ☐

Notes/Insights/Results:

Rate Yourself - Does this trade:

1. Follow system rules?
    1   2   3   4   5

2. Result in fear/anxiety? (If high, why?)
    1   2   3   4   5

3. Spark "greed" or pride?
    1   2   3   4   5

TRADE CHECKLIST & JOURNAL

Date:	Symbol:	Trade Type:

Is this a counter-trend trade? YES ☐ NO ☐   Trigger:

+ Supporting Evidence +	**– Opposing Evidence –**

Heads Up:

Entry Plan		**Exit Plan**	
Entry Order Price:		Technical Stop:	
Max Stop Price:		Exit Target/Trigger:	
Size:		Time Stop:	
Max $ Loss		Est. Risk/Reward:	

Orders/Alerts Placed?   YES ☐   NO ☐   Notes/Insights/Results:

Rate Yourself - Does this trade:

1. Follow system rules?

   1   2   3   4   5

2. Result in fear/anxiety? (If high, why?)

   1   2   3   4   5

3. Spark "greed" or pride?

   1   2   3   4   5

TRADE CHECKLIST & JOURNAL

Date:	Symbol:	Trade Type:

Is this a counter-trend trade?   YES ☐   NO ☐   Trigger:

+ Supporting Evidence +	- Opposing Evidence -

Heads Up:

Entry Plan		Exit Plan	
Entry Order Price:		Technical Stop:	
Max Stop Price:		Exit Target/Trigger:	
Size:		Time Stop:	
Max $ Loss		Est. Risk/Reward:	

Orders/Alerts Placed?   YES ☐   NO ☐   Notes/Insights/Results:

Rate Yourself - Does this trade:

1. Follow system rules?

   1   2   3   4   5

2. Result in fear/anxiety? (If high, why?)

   1   2   3   4   5

3. Spark "greed" or pride?

   1   2   3   4   5

TRADE CHECKLIST & JOURNAL

Date:	Symbol:	Trade Type:

Is this a counter-trend trade?   YES ☐   NO ☐ | Trigger:

+ Supporting Evidence +	- Opposing Evidence -

Heads Up:

Entry Plan		Exit Plan	
Entry Order Price:		Technical Stop:	
Max Stop Price:		Exit Target/Trigger:	
Size:		Time Stop:	
Max $ Loss		Est. Risk/Reward:	

Orders/Alerts Placed?   YES ☐   NO ☐ | Notes/Insights/Results:

Rate Yourself - Does this trade:

1. Follow system rules?

   1   2   3   4   5

2. Result in fear/anxiety? (If high, why?)

   1   2   3   4   5

3. Spark "greed" or pride?

   1   2   3   4   5

"Profits take care of themselves, but losses never do."

JESSE LIVERMORE

TRADE LOG

Symbol	Date Entry	Trade Type	Open Price	Close Price	#	Date Exit	Gain/Loss	Trigger or Note

"If at first you don't succeed, you're normal." MICHAEL HYATT

TRADE LOG

Symbol	Date Entry	Trade Type	Open Price	Close Price	#	Date Exit	Gain/Loss	Trigger or Note

"Insight without action is worthless." PHIL MCGRAW

TRADE LOG

Symbol	Date Entry	Trade Type	Open Price	Close Price	#	Date Exit	Gain/Loss	Trigger or Note

"Obstacles are those frightful things you see when you take your eyes off your goal." HENRY FORD

TRADE LOG

Symbol	Date Entry	Trade Type	Open Price	Close Price	#	Date Exit	Gain/Loss	Trigger or Note

"It is good to repeat and review what is good twice and thrice over." PLATO

TRADE LOG

Symbol	Date Entry	Trade Type	Open Price	Close Price	#	Date Exit	Gain/Loss	Trigger or Note

"Men's expectations manifest in trends." JOHN W HENRY

TRADE LOG

Symbol	Date Entry	Trade Type	Open Price	Close Price	#	Date Exit	Gain/Loss	Trigger or Note

"It is a capital mistake to theorize before one has data." SIR ARTHUR CONAN DOYLE

"Trading skills are developed over time. The task is to survive until you make it!"

DENNIS WILBORN

LESSONS – NOTES – REVIEW

Use this section for anything notable: lessons from, or thoughts about your overall trading execution or performance, doodling your favorite chart patterns, system details you might change going forward, any training or educational resources you want to take advantage of, ways you can manage the emotional rollercoaster trading can bring, etc.

"Losing an illusion makes you wiser than finding a truth." LUDWIG BORNE

LESSONS – NOTES – REVIEW

"The greatest geniuses sometimes accomplish more when they work less." LEONARDO DA VINCI

LESSONS – NOTES – REVIEW

"Often our trading attitudes become a reflection of our life attitudes. They come into our trading because of who we are before we started trading!" DENNIS WILBORN

LESSONS – NOTES – REVIEW

"Life can only be understood backwards; but it must be lived forwards." SØREN KIERKEGAARD

RESOURCES

FREE RESOURCES

- Get free watch lists, reports, and market analysis at https://ActiveTrendTrading.com
- Free tools mentioned in this journal https://ActiveTrendTrading.com/attsfreesignup

TRAINING & TRADE ALERTS

- *Active Trend Trading Premium Membership* – Premium watch lists, live webinar training, and live trade alerts by text and email. Find out more at https://ActiveTrendTrading.com/membership

MENTORING

- *Accelerate Mentoring* – Active Trend Trading's 6-week personalized jump start to help new and experienced traders get to the next level of consistent success. Learn more at http://bit.ly/ATTSMentoring

SOCIAL MEDIA

- *How to Make Money Trading Stocks* YouTube channel – http://bit.ly/ATTSYouTube
- Facebook – https://www.facebook.com/ActiveTrendTrading

"If you think education is expensive, try ignorance." DEREK BOK